T0331759

HANDBOOK OF DIGITAL ENTERPRISE SYSTEMS

Digital Twins, Simulation and AI

HANDBOOK OF DIGITAL ENTERPRISE SYSTEMS

Digital Twins, Simulation and AI

Wolfgang Kühn

University of Wuppertal, Germany

World Scientific

NEW JERSEY · LONDON · SINGAPORE · BEIJING · SHANGHAI · HONG KONG · TAIPEI · CHENNAI · TOKYO

Published by

World Scientific Publishing Co. Pte. Ltd.

5 Toh Tuck Link, Singapore 596224

USA office: 27 Warren Street, Suite 401-402, Hackensack, NJ 07601

UK office: 57 Shelton Street, Covent Garden, London WC2H 9HE

British Library Cataloguing-in-Publication Data
A catalogue record for this book is available from the British Library.

HANDBOOK OF DIGITAL ENTERPRISE SYSTEMS
Digital Twins, Simulation and AI

ISBN 978-981-120-073-1

For any available supplementary material, please visit
https://www.worldscientific.com/worldscibooks/10.1142/11290#t=suppl

Printed in Singapore

Dedication

To the reader …

The future is starting now and digital is at the heart of enterprise strategies. This book shall give you some ideas about information technology, Digital Twins and Artificial Intelligence in digital enterprises. I hope the book helps you to focus on your priorities and to develop ideas on how to adapt strategies that are always agile towards changing future demands.

Finally, I would like to thank my wife Ruth Kuehn-Loewe for supporting me unconditionally with love and patience during the time of writing this book. Thanks, it is a privilege to share my life and love with you.

Preface

Digitalization is changing everything rapidly. Products and industries are getting more innovative and more data-centric and involve more software than ever. Industrial enterprises are moving towards digitally driven enterprises and decision-making is increasingly the most important factor in success. This book is intended to give the reader a fundamental idea and an overview of digital enterprises, the related decision-making and information technologies. Cloud and edge computing, the Industrial Internet of Things, Digital Twins, or virtual clones of physical assets, machine learning and advanced methods of Artificial Intelligence and agile methods are briefly described. In digital enterprises decision-making is increasingly moving from pure human-based decision-making towards decision-making with the use of artificial intelligence. This will have an impact on organization, jobs and learning as well. During the last three years, things have moved fast and the speed of the changes is increasing. Due to these rapid changes, the book uses actual information available through the internet, mostly from various industrial players. Nowadays the half-life period of knowledge is decreasing and the ability to deal with changes will become increasingly more important in all areas of life and business. To be a disrupter, rather than being disrupted, requires one to develop visions and to turn these systematically into successful business reality. If the book can help the reader to move in this direction, the goal of the book will be achieved.

Prof. Dr.-Ing. Wolfgang Kuehn

Contents

List of Figures

Chapter 1

Introduction

"The Digital Economy is here. And if you don't believe it, it's already too late for you." (Lucas 2016a)

The future is now and digitalization changes everything rapidly. We are living in a digitally disrupted world (Behrendt *et al.* 2017, p. 15) and digitalization changes daily lives as well as existing business models. On the other hand, digitalization creates new business opportunities. Products from all industries are getting more innovative and more data-centric and involve more software than ever before. The Internet of Things (IoT) connectivity becomes an integral component and the next generation of smart products will be more complex. With the Industrial Internet of Things (IIoT) the industrial environment is becoming more connected as intelligent devices and machines generate massive amounts of data. Through real-time interfaces a bridge between the real and virtual worlds becomes reality. Turning data into value is increasingly a key success factor.

Further globalization creates new opportunities and disrupts existing markets through extended international supply networks and collaborative partnerships. Globalization requires distributed modular enterprise structures. The evolution of business environments is proceeding rapidly and the fast changes in information technology open up new challenges for business environments and production or logistic processes. Smart factories with smarter, faster and cheaper robots along with additive manufacturing processes are moving rapidly into the industrial field and are leading the industry towards digital enterprises.

Over the last years there has been a revolution of technologies such as mobile, social media and big data. Others such as Artificial Intelligence are just at the beginning. These changes towards digitalization are creating new opportunities and new business use cases. The world is becoming more interconnected as the IIoT is linking huge amounts of devices and automating processes. The cost of sensors, network hardware, computing power, data storage and communication bandwidth have fallen significantly during the last few years and at the same time the system performance has been improved. By 2020 approximately more than 20 billion items will be connected and most major business processes and systems will incorporate some element of the IIoT. (Gerber 2017) As a consequence, rich data, ubiquitous connectivity and real-time communication are changing the way enterprises work (Gupta and Ulrich 2017, p. 33).

Digital transformation is an essential driver of revenue, profit and growth. It is no longer a choice and will determine the future of business. Digital transformation cannot be incremental or considered independently from the operating model (Siemens 2018a). In order to remain ahead of the competition, leading companies increase their investment in cloud computing and enterprise mobility, in the Industrial Internet of Things (IIoT) technology, in Big Data analytics, in Machine Learning and Artificial Intelligence (SAP 2017). A successful digital transformation across the enterprise, which is extended to partners and suppliers, will be a key factor for future success.

Digital Twins are a very important approach to running advanced digital enterprises. Digital Twins are virtual clones of real assets (Fig. 1.1), which sense and analyze data, create insights and feed these back towards the real assets in order to act and improve decision making. Capturing real-time sensor data from connected devices enables us to enrich sensor data with business and contextual data. These data are analyzed on an ongoing basis to identify insights. These insights are leveraged to transform the real system. Digital Twins offer us the opportunity to better understand systems, to continuously improve products, processes, services and even to identify new business models that give us a competitive advantage (Kaiser 2016).

Digital Twins can cover the entire lifecycle of an asset or process by forming a foundation for a closed-loop value chain for smart, connected products, services and production or logistic processes, from design to production, from deployment to continuous improvement. The continuous improvement is increasingly important to integrate digital technologies.

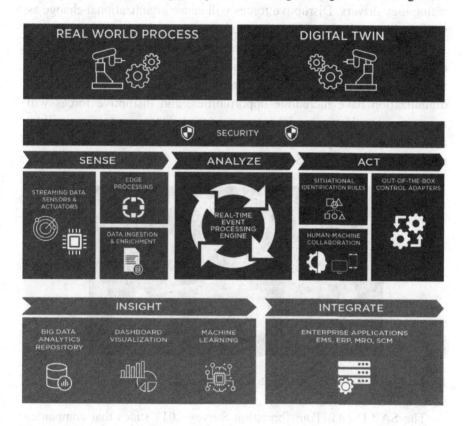

Fig. 1.1. Digital Twin Concept (Pronier 2018).

The concept of the Digital Twin (Fig. 1.1), completes the knowledge loop from design and testing to production and operation and from data acquisition and analytics to improved service and then back again (Siemens 2018b).

An analysis of McKinsey in 2018 states that the industrial sector will see more disruption within the next five years than it has in the past 20 years (Dhawan *et al.* 2018, p. 6) and of course this will not be the end of the story. No part of modern manufacturing and logistic organization will remain untouched by the digital transformation and to survive disruption, companies must rethink all aspects of their business models and their approaches to competitors and take advantage of new and disruptive technology drivers. Disruptive forces will cause organizational change as well as changes in the technology used (McKinsey 2018, p. 11).

The disruptive nature of digitalization opens up new business opportunities and makes it possible to satisfy customer requirements more efficiently (Siemens 2018c). Enterprises that can capitalize on digitalization have incredible opportunities, and disruptive forces will raise revenues. However, not every industrial sector or company will be able to adapt quickly enough and not all leading players will retain their positions (McKinsey 2018, p. 7).

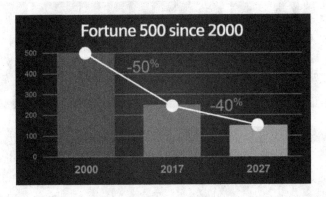

Fig. 1.2. Fortune 500 Companies Which Have Disappeared since 2000 (Siemens 2018a).

The SAP Digital Transformation Survey 2017 states that companies treating digital transformation just as another IT project will not just fall behind, but will fail (SAP 2017, p. 3). Digital is the main reason that over half of the Fortune 500 companies have disappeared since 2000 and it is estimated that digital disruption will wipe out another 40 percent in the next decade (Siemens 2018d). Leading companies report a high level of investment in modern information technologies, such as cloud computing, enterprise mobility, Big Data and analytics, the Industrial Internet of Things (IIoT), Machine Learning and Artificial Intelligence. These leading companies already earn higher profits and revenues and have more competitive differentiation, an advantage that will continue into the future. These companies expect 23% more revenue growth from digital transformation over the next two years compared to the average company (SAP 2017).

1.1 Industrial Revolution

There have been many changes in industries during the last century. But the speed of change is rapidly increasing.

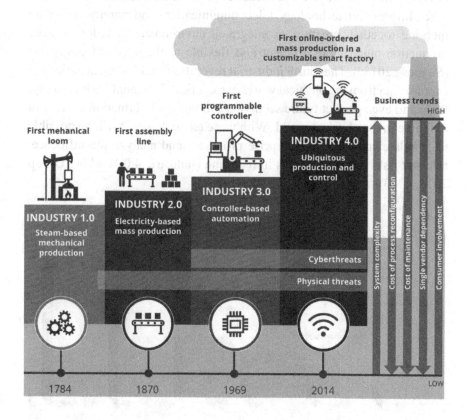

Fig. 1.3. Industrial Revolution (Cotteleer and Sniderman 2017, p. 3).

The first industrial revolution started in the late 18th century and was based on mechanization with the advent of steam power and the invention of the power loom (Fig. 1.3). The first industrial revolution radically changed how products were manufactured. The second industrial revolution started in the late 19th century with electricity and assembly lines for mass production. The third industrial revolution in the 1970s focused on computing and automation.

The fourth industrial revolution integrates physical and digital technologies such as analytics, cognitive technologies, the Industrial Internet of Things (IIoT) and Artificial Intelligence. A huge number of devices will communicate and exchange information in real time with each other. Information technology, telecommunications and manufacturing are merging together, creating an integrated environment in order to make production much more efficient and flexible to the needs of customers (Siemens 2018e). The fourth industrial revolution enables organizations to capture data from the physical world in a cyclical flow, analyze it digitally, learn and even predict future scenarios and use the information to react in real time in the physical world. With these technologies it will be possible to simulate steps in the enterprise processes and analyze the influence, relevant risks and alternatives in real time (Industrie 4.0 Working Group 2013, p. 73).

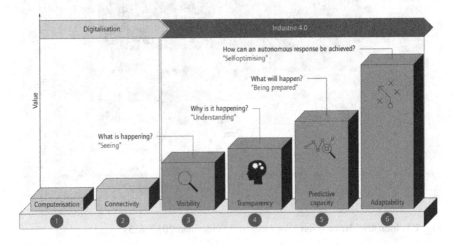

Fig. 1.4. Industry 4.0 Development Path (Schuh *et al.* 2017, p. 16).

The first stage in the Industry 4.0 development path (Fig. 1.4), has been computerization. Computerization offers isolated applications for singular devices and processes. In the second stage the isolated deployment of information technology has been replaced by connected components, which provide connectivity and interoperability. In stage three, sensors offer large amounts of real-time data from devices and processes. This enables us to develop up-to-date digital models (Digital Twin / digital shadow / digital clone) of devices or factories at all times. These Digital Twins can visualize what is going on in the system at any time, in order to improve management decisions based on real-time data. In stage four the Digitals Twins help to understand why things are happening. This understanding can be used to produce engineering knowledge by means of data-based analyses. In the fifth stage Digital Twins can be used to simulate different future scenarios and to identify the most likely ones. In the sixth stage certain decisions are delegated to Artificial Intelligence systems in order to adapt processes quickly to changing environments. The goal of adaptability has been achieved when systems are able to gain the best possible results automatically in real-time (Schuh *et al.* 2017, p. 15).

Organizations take advantage of network, autonomous and cognitive technologies in order to be more responsive regarding unexpected and unpredictable shifts. Virtual twins, machine learning, Artificial Intelligence and other advanced technologies are developed to improve enterprise operation. Systems connecting embedded system production technologies and smart production processes are also described as Cyber-Physical Systems. Besides the technical change it is crucial to understand the important relationship between business, workforce productivity, financial outcomes and innovative strategies and social needs and people's feeling of stability and well-being (Sniderman *et al.* 2016). These cyber-physical systems also extend to asset management for predictive maintenance, statistical evaluation and measurements to increase asset reliability (Favilla *et al.* 2018, p. 2).

The fourth industrial revolution has been started and the concept of digitizing everything is increasingly becoming reality. The details and diverse aspects of these changes and the impact for future developments of digital enterprises shall be discussed in this book.

1.2 Digital Challenge and Transformation

Digitalization is already changing every aspect of life and existing business models. Technological disruption in the industrial business world has increased significantly. The increasing maturity of analytics and the IoT is leading industrial businesses to interconnect products, value chains and business models (Butner *et al.* 2017, p. 3). Digital transformation is directly related to a changing digital economy, with individuals, businesses and society becoming interconnected in real-time, supported by technology (IDC 2017, p. 2).

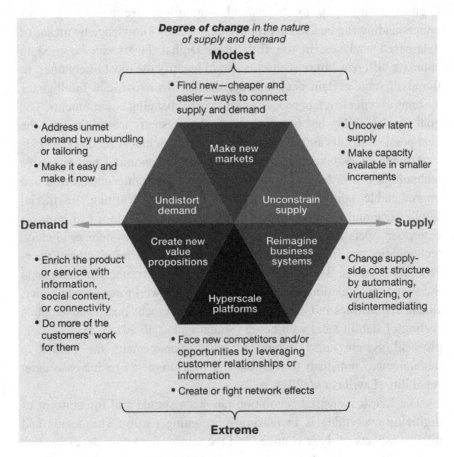

Fig. 1.5. Disruption of Industries by Digitization (Dawson *et al.* 2016, p. 4).

Digitalization enables industries to turn product ideas into reality in new ways by drawing on technological trends like generative design and intelligent models. The use of cloud solutions and knowledge automation is changing industries, and additive manufacturing and advanced robotics is leading production in an innovative direction (Siemens 2018c).

During the last few years digitalization has changed all areas of private life and business reality. And this is only the beginning. Existing business models have to be adapted, in order to be competitive in response to future demands. This increases pressure on industries and also opens up new business opportunities at the same time. For modern enterprises there is a need to develop into a digital enterprise in order to stay ahead of the competition. Digital disruptions (Fig. 1.6), are happening faster than ever. Digitalization requires us to behave flexibly and to develop new business models faster than competitors in order to be successful and to survive. Typical drivers for IIoT utilization are improving operational efficiency, boosting productivity, improving customer satisfaction, increasing revenues, facilitating product innovation, optimizing operations, gaining a competitive edge, reducing operating cost and creating new jobs (Bourne 2018, p. 7).

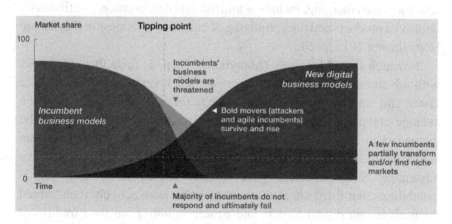

Fig. 1.6. Digital Disruptions (Bughin *et al.* 2018, p. 6).

Digital technologies are creating entirely new business opportunities and challenges. On the other hand, digitalization is also eroding traditional barriers to entry in many sectors, enabling the development of entirely new categories of products and creating new alternatives for customers (Behrendt *et al.* 2017, p. 18). With digitalization, products are changing into smart products and manufacturing into smart manufacturing. The next-generation of smart products will be complex systems that make current development processes inadequate. Smart factories with smarter, faster and cheaper robots along with additive manufacturing processes are disrupting factories and transforming manufacturing industries. Smart products require a new model-based design approach and improved manufacturing approaches. Global teams across all disciplines have to share the detailed information required in order to evaluate opportunities and predict performance (Siemens 2018f).

Smart, connected products are forcing companies to undergo a radical shift, to redefine and rethink nearly everything. The unprecedented data and new capabilities that smart, connected products provide are changing interactions with customers into new relationships which are continuous and open-ended. New processes are required, as are reshaping nearly every function in the value chain and more intense coordination among functions. For cross-functional collaboration, entirely new functions and structures are emerging, including unified data organization, continuously improved products and the optimizing of customer relationship (Porter and Heppelmann 2015, p. 5).

Research from McKinsey (Manyika 2017, p. 3) finds that companies with advanced digital capabilities grow their revenue and market share faster and improve profit margins three times more rapidly than the average company. Often these have been the fastest innovators and the disruptors in specific fields. Compared with these leaders, the rest are significantly behind in using digital capabilities for competitive advantage. Some of these have already started using their digital capabilities, but there are also companies that have actively transformed themselves into digital leaders and benefit doubly from their traditional strengths and their new digital capabilities.

Digitalization is affecting every industry, disrupting current leaders and creating new business opportunities. Enterprises have to deal with constantly increasing complexity in products and manufacturing with reduced cycle times and decreased yield. To survive disruption, manufacturers must rethink every aspect of the business, move towards a digital enterprise and take advantage of new and disruptive technology drivers in order to create new business opportunities.

Digitization will become a key part of all the activities of the company in the future. All the technologies needed for data analysis, data-driven services, connectivity and cyber-security have to be connected. This digitization will generate major synergies. New digital technology opens new business models, which in turn give rise to new and potentially disruptive market entrants. This shift is accelerating in every industry and compelling every established organization to transform itself into a digital enterprise with the goal of not only surviving, but thriving in the new social and business reality (Lucas 2016a). If policy makers and businesses get it right, linking the physical and digital worlds could generate up to $11.1 trillion a year in economic value by 2025 (Menard 2018, p. 32).

However, successful transformation requires digital innovation strategies to create comprehensive and precise digital models of products and production operations to manage the complexity of smart products and smart production operations. With these strategies, companies can have the power and flexibility to speed up development, optimize manufacturing and use the insight gained from product and plant operations to improve future performance (Siemens 2018a). Digital transformation combines multiple digital technologies including cloud, cognitive, mobile and IoT to reconceive customer and partner relationships and operations (Butner *et al.* 2017, p. 5).

Digital transformation is directly related to the changing digital economy, with individuals, businesses and society becoming interconnected in real-time, supported by technology. The business requirement for organizations and data is critical in executing this transformation, enabling innovation and competitive differentiation. Data-driven organizations have better decision-making abilities with an immediate positive impact, but managing data is a hot challenge. Digital transformation requires robust and suitable data architecture with strong governance not only to maintain security but also to enable activities such as analytics, enterprise, connecting objects and Artificial Intelligence.

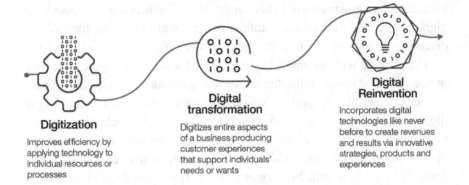

Digitization

Improves efficiency by
applying technology to
individual resources or
processes

Digital
transformation

Digitizes entire aspects
of a business producing
customer experiences
that support individuals'
needs or wants

Digital
Reinvention

Incorporates digital
technologies like never
before to create revenues
and results via innovative
strategies, products and
experiences

Fig. 1.7. Digital Reinvention Path (Butner *et al.* 2017, p. 6).

There is a path from digitalization through Digital Transformation to Digital Reinvention (Fig. 1.7). Digital Reinvention differs in concept from the digitization of individual capabilities or functions and the process of digitally transforming major business processes or activities. Digital Reinvention goes much further and combines multiple digital technologies including cloud, cognitive, mobile and IIoT to reconceive customer and partner relationships and operations.

It relies on a range of digital applications and technologies and involves fundamentally reimagining the way a business operates and engages with its stakeholders. Digital Reinvention requires rethinking how an enterprise operates and how it engages with its partners, customers and its environment as a whole (Butner *et al*. 2017, p. 6). The extent of Digitization varies by company, with a large gap between digital leaders and the rest (Manyika 2017, p. 3). Digitalization, Digital Transformation and Digital Reinvention are processes, not destinations, to improve efficiency and competitive positions, which consider technology and also a strong participation of the management.

1.3 Digital Enterprises

Industrial enterprises have to deal with global industrial operations regarding engineering, optimization and operations (Fig. 1.8). In industrial enterprises the demands for improved product performance, production flexibility and reduced operating cost are the driving forces of innovation. This is facilitated by collaborative program management across the product lifecycle and the supply network throughout the entire product lifecycle. Enterprises have to respond flexibly and effectively to changing production schedules, which are made more challenging due to the requirements of global supply networks. Due to increasing global competition, rapidly changing markets, growing complexity and the variation of markets and consumer demands, industrial enterprises need to reduce time-to-market, time-to-volume and time-to-customer significantly.

At the same time, they must enhance flexibility, improve quality, increase efficiency, reduce energy and resource consumption and also establish cyber security (Fig. 1.9). Further products have to be sustainable, environmentally friendly and energy efficient in manufacturing. And production is becoming an increasingly important competitive advantage.

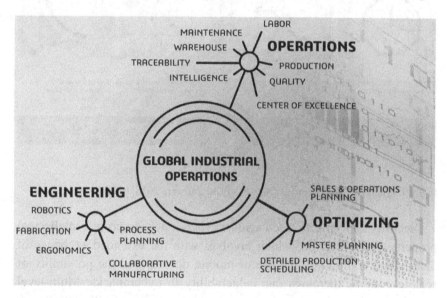

Fig. 1.8. Global Industrial Operations (Dassault Systèmes 2017a).

Enterprises have to launch products with increasing complexity faster (time-to-market), ensure a fast and safe start of production (time-to-volume) und deliver the products using an optimized supply chain (time-to-customer). This requires the integration and optimization of product development, production or logistics planning and control. Nowadays the fast competitor beats the slow one. Consumers request for individualized products, but at the prices of mass-produced goods. As a consequence, production has to become more flexible.

Quality is essential to satisfy customers. Consumers reward makers of high quality goods and punish makers of poor quality goods by use of the internet. Digitalization makes it possible to improve quality and to manufacture with top quality right away. In the global competition the increase of efficiency is mandatory. This requires the reduction of planning costs and the avoidance of planning errors and at the same time the reduction of production costs. Through the standardization of solutions and the increase of productivity the costs can be reduced.

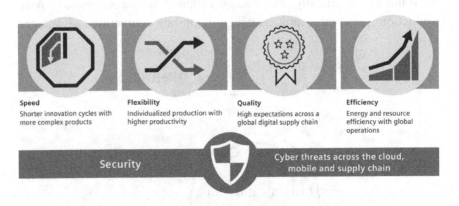

Fig. 1.9. Enterprise Requirements (Siemens PLM Software 2018, p. 3).

Security concepts are used against cyber-attacks to protect intellectual property. Digitalization, which involves with the extended exchange of data, cloud computing, the use of mobile devices and the possibility of remote control, increases our vulnerability to cyberattacks. Multi-level security concepts must meet these challenges (Siemens PLM Software 2018, p. 3). To achieve these goals manufacturers are forced to rethink their source-make-deliver processes, depending on their target market locations, requirements and conditions. They do go through the closer integration of manufacturing operations over the complete value chain.

Industrial enterprises are moving towards Digital Enterprises (Fig. 1.10), which incorporate digital technology as a competitive advantage for all internal and external operations. Digital enterprises are offering integrated approaches to enhance products, services and all processes. Within the digital enterprise, simulation technology as a key factor is applied in virtual models on various planning, control and operational levels, in order to improve products and processes. Digital Enterprises are not something to introduce for technology purposes. Transforming a business into a digital enterprise will enable the business to produce better services, products and outcomes for the customers, much faster and of course at lower costs (Lucas 2016a).

Organizations with a modern digital enterprise platform will be more agile and responsive to customers than their competitors. However, as organizations begin the transformation process to become a digital enterprise, the starting point, and also the core technology and infrastructure, which a company runs, have to be considered.

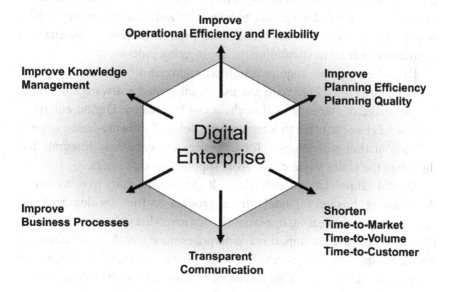

Fig. 1.10. Goals of the Digital Enterprises.

New and innovative technologies and processes have to achieve increased efficiency, performance and flexibility to compete successfully. The focus is on managing complex programs, synchronizing global design and development with virtual environments. Aligning the supply chain meets dynamic production schedules, compressing development cycles and deploying faster and more efficient manufacturing and assembly processes. Virtual models which minimize virtual prototyping assembly errors and design rework and reduce cycle times for maintenance and repair. In order to realize sustainable profit and growth, business success will be determined by the ability to transform investments into dynamic, secure and seamless digital environments that can integrate operations into a highly functional, global value chain.

Digital enterprises focus on affordability, asset visibility and supply network efficiency. A seamless, collaborative business environment has to support the entire design-to-manufacturing process to enable access and utilize data throughout the lifecycle. Real-time configuration control and observance of security processes and procedures guarantees adherence to infrastructure and data standards. The costs and risks of using advanced materials and technologies have to be minimized. Innovative engineering accelerates the design of the product and production process by enabling team collaboration to streamline the engineering processes.

Digital enterprises require a holistic approach to optimize the entire value chain (Fig. 1.11). With the use of integrated software solutions a digital image of the entire value chain can be created. Digital enterprise approaches have to offer an integrated portfolio of software-based systems and automation technologies for industries to seamlessly integrate and digitalize the entire value chain, from suppliers to customers.

Digitalization changes everything. It changes the daily lives as well as the existing business models from product-centric development and manufacturing to creating opportunities for extended value throughout the lifecycle. To remain competitive, enterprises must transform all phases of business through digitalization using digital software solutions for innovation and growth. This increases pressure on product development and also opens new business opportunities.

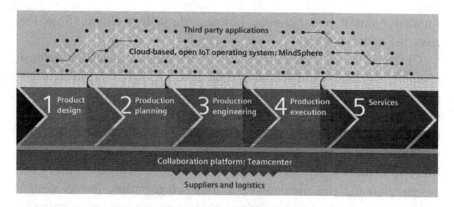

Fig. 1.11. Holistic Approach for the Entire Value Chain (Siemens 2018c).

The digital enterprise approach integrates all aspects of enterprise planning and control. Typical application areas to be covered are Product Lifecycle Management (PLM), Electronic Design Automation (EDA), Product Data Management (PDM), Enterprise Resource Planning (ERP), Manufacturing Operations Management (MOM), Manufacturing Execution Systems (MES), Totally Integrated Automation (TIA), Asset Performance Management (APM), Application Lifecycle Management (ALM) and Customer Relationship Management (CRM).

The digital enterprise concept is not replacing successfully applied manufacturing planning and production concepts such as Supply Network Management, Just in Time Production, Lean Management or Kaizen. These approaches and others can be seen as an integral part to be implemented in the digital enterprise environment.

1.4 About this Book

Chapter 1 briefly describes the span of time from industrial revolution to the digitalization of today. Digitalization is already changing the world and the impact of digital disruption on businesses will increase in future. Production and logistic enterprises have to move towards digital enterprises using advanced information technology to reshape the infrastructure and also the internal and external operations in order to plan, simulate, control and optimize business through networks from the customer to the supplier.

Chapter 2 gives a broad overview of enterprise systems and related planning, simulation and operating approaches. A digital thread connects all areas of the digital enterprise from the customer to the supplier, from integrating product and process engineering, product lifecycle management, enterprise resource planning and manufacturing operations management up to asset performance management and application lifecycle management. On the enterprise planning level approaches for design, planning and simulation are discussed regarding factory design and layout, production and logistics including robotics and automation as well as the impact on human resources, personal digital assistances and augmented reality. On the operational level the focus is on advanced simulation approaches to improve manufacturing operations management. These require a totally integrated automation, which enables real-time interfacing between the physical and digital worlds and delivers data for the advanced planning and simulation approaches and also feedback back to the factory floor. Planning, simulation and advanced controls require enterprise models. Hierarchical enterprise models, defined by the ISA-95 standard and distributed modelling approaches are discussed.

In chapter 3 various aspects of decision-making are described. Decision-making is a very important factor for planning and operating digital enterprises. Based on the requirements for digital enterprises, possible decision-making approaches for decisions by humans as well as machine-based decision-making approaches are discussed. An important issue for the industrial use of machine-based decision-making in practice is the reliability of these processes. The Digital Twin approach, in which a digital clone of the real system is used in a feedback loop for advanced decision-making, is described in detail. Further approaches for enterprise optimization are discussed.

Chapter 4 covers aspects of information technology required for the understanding of digitalization in enterprise systems. The digitalization concepts described in chapter 2 and the decision-making approaches described in chapter 3 require dedicated information technology for industrial use. Cloud computing, edge computing and the Internet of Things are briefly introduced. Due to the specific industrial requirements, such as speed and reliability constraints, a focus is set on the Industrial Internet of Things, interfacing technology and data analytics for industrial purpose. In modern enterprise systems Artificial Intelligence is becoming a more and more important technology. Based on an introduction to machine learning, neuronal networks and deep learning approaches, the opportunities and limitations of using Artificial Intelligence are discussed. Some understanding of the information technologies described in this chapter would be helpful for a deeper understanding of chapter 2 and chapter 3. Depending on the reader's knowledge level regarding information technologies, chapter 4 can also be used to look up some details for better understanding while reading the earlier chapters.

Chapter 5 gives a brief overview on digital enterprise solution software. Due to the rapid changes in the software market this information can give a basic idea about frameworks and architectures available in the market. The described information is a snapshot from solutions available in 2018. Based on this information the reader shall be able to search for information specific to the particular demand. Actual information about particular tools is available on the webpages of the software and system vendors.

In chapter 6 the impact of digitalization in enterprise systems on business models, organization and customer relationships is considered. Digitalization requires changes in management and will have a significant impact on education, jobs, training and learning for everyone involved. Further, in chapter 6 some ideas about future trends regarding enterprise architecture, strategic technology trends and the reliability of predicting future trends are discussed.

Chapter 2

Digital Enterprises

Digitalization is changing the industrial world and customer requests are becoming more and more individualized. To be able to respond appropriately, plant operation has to become more efficient and flexible, with a shorter time-to-market, while maintaining and improving quality. The speed of changes in industries is accelerating. Markets have evolved from organizational centricity, in which manufacturers and service providers largely defined what to produce, towards individual centricity and consumer demand driven markets. These changes are continuing to evolve into new forms, in which customers, clients and colleagues are becoming active participants rather than passive recipients (Butner *et al.* 2017, p. 1).

Digital Enterprises are comprehensive approaches, which consist of the physical industrial enterprise and the integration of data driven virtual enterprises (Fig. 2.1), including Digital Twins. Physical and digital enterprises are connected through real-time data. Digitalization transforms the innovation process into a proactive agent in driving new business opportunities, enabling manufacturers to implement a digital thread through design, realization and execution in order to respond to disruptive innovation and to improve products, processes and services.

Digital Enterprise concepts can be seen as an enterprise and information strategy managing and combining all required processes in global networks. These concepts offer methods and software solutions for product and portfolio planning, digital product development, digital manufacturing, sales and more. Collaborative solutions support the people and processes involved in each product and production phase. Therefore, digital enterprise concepts require data for products and processes, factory modelling, advanced visualization or simulation. Their goal is to improve the quality and dynamic of the products and production processes involved and to deliver faster time-to-value.

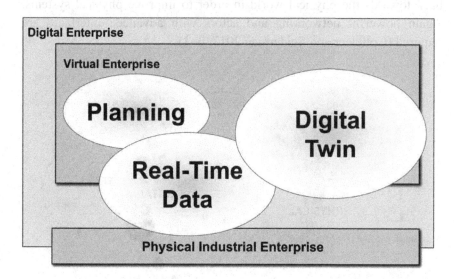

Fig. 2.1. Digital Enterprise.

Digital enterprise concepts include a network of digital models, including visualization, simulation and Artificial Intelligence tools, which are integrated through comprehensive data. Based on actual real-time data in a virtual enterprise, products, resources and processes can be modelled. Based on these data and virtual models the products and processes can be extensively tested, improved and developed mostly error free for use in the physical environment.

The fundamental idea of digital enterprises is to establish a closed loop from the physical world to digital planning and optimization and back to the physical world (Fig. 2.2). The first step (physical to digital) is to capture information from the physical world and create a digital record from physical data. For this many sensor, standardized real-time interfaces and powerful networks are required. The second step (digital to digital) is to share information and uncover meaningful insights using advanced analytics, simulation models, scenario analysis and Artificial

Intelligence. Advanced hard- and software systems have to perform powerful and fast data processing and decision making. The third important step (digital to physical) is to transfer digital-world decisions back towards the physical world in order to improve physical systems. Again powerful networking and actors with advanced interfaces are required (Cotteleer and Sniderman 2017, p. 3).

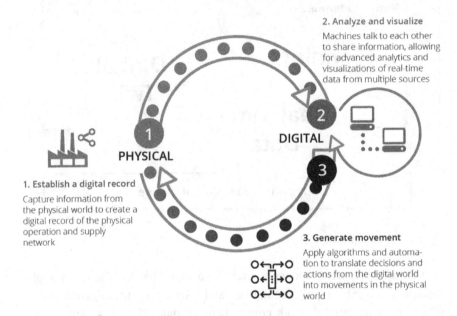

Fig. 2.2. Physical-to-Digital-to-Physical Loop (Cotteleer and Sniderman 2017, p. 3).

The increase of computing power, the improvement of data processing and the availability of real-time data from operating systems and advanced analytics technologies enable us to model in much richer, less isolated and much more sophisticated ways than ever before. This enables us to realize advanced digital enterprise concepts. These concepts require a digital thread as a holistic approach through all areas of a digital enterprise.

2.1 Digital Thread – Holistic Approach

In industrial enterprises the demand for improved product performance, production flexibility and reduced operating costs are a driving force of innovation, facilitated by collaborative program management across the product lifecycle including all related production and logistics processes. Complex production and logistic enterprises have to connect or to integrate various areas in order to improve products and processes on all enterprise levels. A digital thread from the customer to the supplier (Fig. 2.3), has to connect the entire life cycle of a product from design to retirement as well as all business, production and logistic processes involved in digital enterprises.

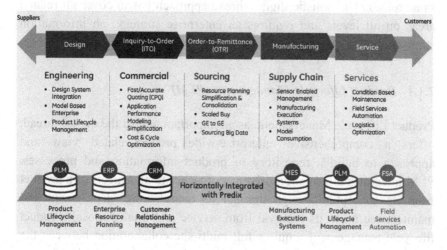

Fig. 2.3. Digital Thread (General Electric Company 2016, p. 25).

Within a digital enterprise a holistic thread has to connect Product Lifecycle Management (PLM), Electronic Design Automation (EDA), Product Data Management (PDM), Enterprise Resource Planning (ERP), Manufacturing Operations Management (MOM), Manufacturing Execution Systems (MES), Totally Integrated Automation (TIA), Total Quality Management (TQM), Asset Performance Management (APM), Application Lifecycle Management (ALM), Customer Relationship Management (CRM) and more. These different approaches always offer a specific view on the enterprise and are partly overlapping. Product Lifecycle Management offers a product related view on the lifecycle of products and all related issues. Enterprise design, planning and simulation have resource related views on the planning of enterprise systems. Manufacturing Operations Management offers an operational view, Totally Integrated Automation a view of the integration from the planning and operational level to the controls on the factory floor and Total Quality Management and Asset Performance Management are cross sectional functions. Customer Relationship Management looks at the business from the marketing and sales point of view. All of these views are not independent. Each offers a special perspective, which may partly overlap with other views or even offer a different view on the same topics. The holistic digital thread approach has to cover all related areas on all levels and requires an enterprise strategy, an information strategy and a transformational business strategy at the same time.

2.1.1 *Product Lifecycle Management (PLM)*

Product Lifecycle Management, as an important part of the digital thread, offers a comprehensive enterprise-wide product-related view and approach to build a repository of product information and processes. PLM integrates information-driven approaches to all aspects of a product from its conceptual design through its manufacture, deployment and maintenance up to its removal from service and final disposal. Product lifecycle management requires full multi-site collaboration between the product and process engineering approaches to integrate the design, automated engineering and manufacturing processes in order to achieve a competitive advantage through improved engineering performance.

PLM, as an important part of the digital thread, represents the product definition, product variants and traceability across the lifecycle. As mechanical, electrical and software components are becoming an integral part of products, PLM solutions must be able to manage the production of increasingly complex products from concept through to end of life (Fig. 2.4). PLM tracks data, processes, decisions and results across the product lifecycle. It provides early decision-making, integrates manufacturing considerations and the ability to trace back in time all inputs, decisions and data across the product lifecycle at various lifecycle stages.

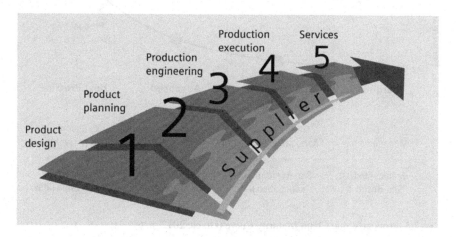

Fig. 2.4. Holistic Approach to Optimize the Entire Value Chain (Siemens 2017a, p. 2).

PLM starts with the concept to build phase. Due to advances in algorithms and simulation technologies many products are already created in advance in a virtual world. The Digital Twin of the physical world counterpart can be tested and optimized in the virtual world. During the design to build phase a detailed design of the product and manufacturing processes has to be performed and decisions regarding the selection of manufacturing processes and tooling have to be made. To meet the requirements, it is essential to consider in parallel the product design reviews and the manufacturing or logistics process design as well. At the plan to build stage, detailed manufacturing planning is performed, which includes capacity planning, detailed plant design, resource allocations and the analysis of complete manufacturing systems. During the build to deliver phase production processes have to be executed efficiently and tracking, management of production, inspection, delivery and service records have to be coordinated.

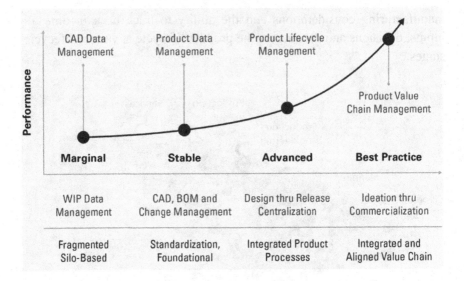

Fig. 2.5. Product Value Chain Maturity Curve (Oracle 2012, p. 6).

In this holistic approach, continuous improvement is essential in order to reach and to maintain excellence. PLM represents a strategic approach to the product value chain that emphasizes process efficiency by cross-functional collaboration in the extended enterprise with rapid innovation and rigorous quality control including risk mitigation and cost-effectiveness. The data management of product relevant data (Fig. 2.5), has developed from the management of CAD-Data to Product Data Management to Product Live Cycle Management, and is now moving towards Product Value Chain Management.

The PLM approach offers us the capability to manage products over the complete lifecycle. The bill of material management organizes and synchronizes multiple sources of information in order to create and maintain structured, multi-level bills of materials for each stage of the product lifecycle including design, manufacturing and support. Parts management provides complete control over the lifecycle of parts, including automated workflows and permissions to help manage the approval processes. Component engineering supports electronic component selection, approval, sourcing and compliance processes and change management capabilities. These provide mechanical, electrical, software and documentation teams with complete visibility into the change status of a product or system.

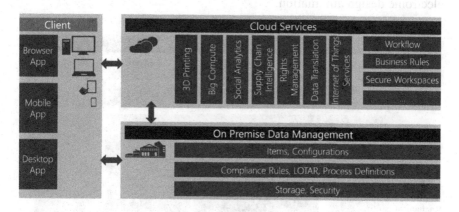

Fig. 2.6. Microsoft Future of PLM (Floyd 2014).

PLM project management facilitates the management of new product development and the engineer-to-order processes for complex projects that require global collaboration. Requirements management enables the creation of a single, multidiscipline requirement hierarchy for managing complex engineering systems including planning, development and realization. Configuration management provides a comprehensive methodology for managing the configuration of a product or system throughout its lifecycle. Document management includes version and change control in a secure, searchable repository. Quality management provides organizations with tools to manage risk, improve quality and attain environmental, regulatory, safety and other forms of compliance, using Advanced Product Quality Planning (APQP) and Failure Mode Effects Analysis (FMEA) to control and mitigate critical product risks to achieve compliance with regulatory requirements and quality standards.

2.1.1.1 *Product and Process Engineering*

To turn ideas into products, innovative engineering requires us to accelerate the design of the product and production processes by enabling team collaboration to streamline engineering processes. In global networks multi-site teams have to manage engineering processes using CAD, CAM and CAE information for mechanical, electrical and electronic design automation.

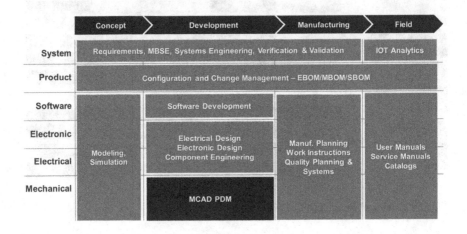

Fig. 2.7. Business of Engineering (Aras 2017, p. 12).

Engineering concepts for digital enterprises require the integration of all steps involved from the concept under development and being manufactured to the field (Fig. 2.7). This includes all levels from mechanical, electrical and electronic to software and systems. Teams have to work effectively together independent of their physical location, synchronizing the engineering processes by integrating CAD designs and CAE information. Their goal is to increase product innovation and flexibility, to catch costly design mistakes up front in the product lifecycle and to accelerate product and service delivery (Aras 2018a, p. 3).

2.1.1.2 *Product Data Management (PDM)*

Product Data Management (PDM) is a subset of Product Lifecycle Management and has to be integrated using CAD and CAE tools to securely manage design data. Associated parts and multidisciplinary Bills of Materials (BOMs) are faced with the increasing challenge of ensuring that all types and data formats of CAD data are accessible to all users involved, regardless of discipline or location. Product Data

Management is the management of the creation, change and archiving of all required product related information, in order to provide clear and secure access to all users. This includes synchronization of the parts and BOMs managing the lifecycle of ECAD and MCAD information. Connectors are required for MCAD, ECAD, ALM and Office-Tools so that they can be integrated with other digital enterprise systems. With the exchange of data across the enterprise, cross-disciplinary change management has to be applied.

2.1.2 *Application Lifecycle Management (ALM)*

Application Lifecycle Management (ALM) is the monitoring of applications over the entire life cycle in order to improve quality and performance. With enterprise digitalization, the topic of ALM is becoming increasingly important. Due to the rapid change of applications, enterprises must adapt existing systems faster and also establish new ones. ALM is intended to shorten the software development life-cycle and to improve the overall quality of the software. Standardization ensures greater efficiency and better cooperation between development teams and users. The overall Application Lifecycle Management process includes the phases of analysis, design, implementation, testing, release and maintenance. A phase model ensures that the individual steps of implementation are observed and continuously checked.

In the initial requirement phase the determination and analysis of requirements have to be performed. Applications are usually oriented to the strategic planning of an enterprise, and in the first phase it is important to understand what will be achieved with the application. The result of this phase is a clear specification defining the contents, implementation guidelines and design drafts and establishing first mock-ups. In the conception phase, the requirements from the first phase are translated into detailed concepts for design and software architecture. The development phase includes the implementation of the application, setting up the development and acceptance environment, developing the software, documentation and installing the solutions in the integration environment. Demand-oriented test scenarios and unit tests shall improve the application development. In the product release phase, the roll-out and training courses take place. The maintenance and optimization phases usually take place in the background while the application is in use and requires a versioning, which ensures the maintainability. Quality assurance is a cross-section functionality which cannot be assigned to a single phase.

2.1.3 *Enterprise Design, Planning and Simulation*

This phase offers a resource-related view of the enterprise. Industrial enterprises are moving towards flexible networking structures, offering flexible relations between employees and resources. Modern productions will move towards information-centric factories, in which Artificial Intelligence-driven self-organizing structures will operate holistically. Flexible robot assistants and additive or subtractive manufacturing systems are parts of optimizing the flows of materials and energy. The decentralizing of functions using peer-to-peer communication offers the flexibility required for problem-solving. Due to the market approach, enterprise resources shall be allocated on request. The allocation of many resources has to be decided flexibly on demand. Planning and operation have to be performed in nearly real time. Flexible decision-making using advanced information technologies is required for situation-driven decisions to move towards self-organizing systems. An open environment which can generate situation-driven decisions can create new knowledge to improve the enterprise. The use of simulation models and Artificial Intelligence techniques enables dynamic analysis to meet the demands for efficient operations.

The style in which enterprise design, planning and simulation is performed will change in near future. For instance, once a product has been created in the virtual world, its data will be seamlessly transferred to production facilities where humans, assisted by semi-autonomous robots, will use additive and subtractive manufacturing methods to automatically translate the virtual model into physical objects. The production can be simulated in real time and the model behavior can be compared with the actual system performance in order to continuously improve quality and predictive maintenance (Siemens 2018b). This kind of enterprise design and planning requires new approaches including advanced simulation and Artificial Intelligence approaches.

2.1.3.1 *Factory Design and Layout*

Industrial enterprises require the creation of efficient factory layouts with reduced part travel distances, lot sizes and inventory levels in order to increase production or logistic efficiency and decrease manufacturing costs. The goals of optimizing the factory flow are to reduce material handling costs, to optimize space utilization of shop floor storage areas and also to promote resource utilization and material flow, to reduce non-value-added work and to minimize indirect labor costs. Factory design, layout and implementation have to be improved in terms of quality and speed in order to meet future demands. Material flow simulation provides alternative layout configurations in order to improve production efficiency.

For factory layout planning, modern software tools are available that enable us to establish virtual 3D-factory layouts and models using predefined modules. By using parametric objects and system toolkits factory models can be created much faster than in traditional 3D-modeling. The simulation of design and layout can be used to discover and resolve problems early in the layout process. Layout information can then be re-used with smart objects.

Virtual reality models enable us to move through factory mock-ups, walk through factories and inspect and animate motion in a rendered 3D-factory model. The digital factory approach allows to integrate data from development and all processes of the value chain. Further simulation offers a powerful platform to improve open and transparent communication between all parties involved in the planning process. Critical issues can be discussed and checked in advance and the improved reliability of planning saves time and money.

2.1.3.2 *Process Planning, Logistics and Material Flow*

Due to digitalization and globalization with increased time pressures and requirements the production logistics becomes an increasingly important aspect for the success of industrial enterprises. Production processes and logistics simulation aim to reduce system costs, to increase existing system productivity, to optimize resource consumption, to reduce inventories and throughput time and to optimize systems regarding energy consumption. Plant, line and process simulation can be performed by means of discrete event simulation. Simulation allows us to analyze systems and processes in order to improve material flow, resource utilization and logistics in all levels of the planning process.

Fig. 2.8. Process Planning (Siemens 2018g).

Numerous production factors affect the operational efficiency and throughput of manufacturing operations, such as the determination of the optimal configuration for new production systems, the establishment of proper levels of work-in-process inventory and the management of appropriate production schedules. Managing global production networks requires advanced decision-making criteria as one is required to invest, evaluate and improve alternative approaches. Simulation models enable us to run experiments virtually and perform what-if scenarios without disturbing an existing production system. The introduction of Just-in-time (JIT) delivery, just-in-sequence (JIS), Kanban controls or other production strategies can be considered. It is also possible to explore system characteristics and optimize the performance of the planned production and logistic systems long before an actual system is built and production is ramped up. Especially for enterprise systems with complex system dynamics, JIT requirements and extreme peak loads, the simulation approach offers large benefits.

Discrete event simulation models enable the analysis of logistic processes, improving resource utilization and logistics on all levels of manufacturing planning from that used in local plants and specific lines to that used in global enterprise facilities in advance. Logistics systems and processes can be modeled and simulated in order to analyze and visualize production throughput and performance. This can be done by checking for bottlenecks, validating transported materials and viewing resource utilization over time for multiple process alternatives in order to improve and optimize system performance.

2.1.3.3 *Robotics and Automation*

Process automation is nothing new. Enterprises have always been looking for ways to achieve improved operating efficiencies and robots have been around for a long time in manufacturing. But now much more flexible, safer and less expensive robots have been developed which engage in service activities and improve over time. Advances in software, Artificial Intelligence, machine learning and innovative technology platforms enable businesses to redefine processes.

Workplace automation is expected to provide significant opportunities for the improvement of performance and efficiency. Artificial Intelligence is starting to improve activities that were previously assumed to require human judgment and experience. A successful automation effort requires a strategic automation concept, deploying technologies systematically (Edlich *et al.* 2018, p. 2). The improved production efficiency and flexibility in the optimization of automation systems and robotic work cells require the simulation of design, logistics and kinematics.

Fig. 2.9. Robotic Spot-Welding (Kuka).

Digital manufacturing and the simulation of robotic applications, from single robot stations to advanced production cells and lines, have to including tooling and peripherals. Based on 3D kinematics simulation (Fig. 2.10), complex robotic systems can do automatic path planning, collision detection, offline programming and robot calibration to improve accuracy. Simulation, analysis, optimization and the offline programming of robotic work cells and automated manufacturing processes require a concurrent engineering platform.

The integration of event-based robotics simulation and offline programming within a data-managed environment allows us to manage, validate and optimize complex production systems in a 6D dynamic environment, including 3 dimension translative and 3 dimension rotatory degrees of movement. High-end motion control systems are required to control modern flexible production systems, covering aspects from speed control over distributed synchronous operation to complex path interpolation.

Fig. 2.10. Kinematic Robotic Simulation (Siemens 2018g).

During the enterprise design phase collaborative simulation tools can reduce the need for physical prototypes through virtual validation, optimizing cycle times through simulation and virtual validation mechanical and electrical systems, components and processes. The collaboration among mechanical design engineers and controls engineers is forced. Virtual twins, simulating the physical and control characteristics of robots and other devices, are used to perform accessibility checks, collision detection, optimization of cycle time and offline programming. This requires an accurate simulation of robot motion and specific controller characteristics, including motion and process parameters.

Recent developments in robotics, Artificial Intelligence and machine learning include a movement from robotic process automation to complex process information and intelligent process automation (Fig. 2.11). In a new automation age, technology performs tasks, which could be done in the past by humans only. These tasks are increasingly performed at a "superhuman" level of performance (Manyika *et al.* 2017,

p. 23). Actually, there are two genres of automation tools emerging, which have the potential to make processes smarter and more efficient. Robotic Process Automation (RPA) has been maturing quietly over the last decade. It is used for enterprise-scale deployments and Intelligent Automation (IA) enabled by cognitive technologies, and is moving into enterprises with increasing transformative potential in the near future.

Intelligent automation continuum

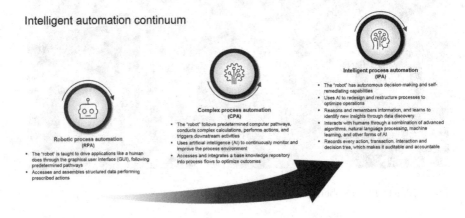

Fig. 2.11. Intelligent Automation Continuum (Williams and Allen 2017, p. 4).

Significant advancements in AI are enabling a new generation of collaborative and context-aware robots. These are flexible, non-special-purpose robots that need less configuration time and are easier to incorporate into specific environments. The robustness of robots in unprepared environments as well as the flexibility of robotic systems has increased significantly. The collaboration between the human workforce and context-aware robots is increasing, especially in assembly-heavy applications. This includes an environment shared by robots and humans with no fenced-in, robots-only areas (McKinsey 2017a, p. 26).

Deep learning is used to correctly identify an object and its position. This enhances flexibility and enables the handling of objects without requiring fixed or predefined positions. AI-enhanced logistics robots are taught how to recognize empty shelf space via camera automatically, leading to a significant speed advantage in picking objects over conventional methods. AI-enhanced logistic robots are also able to integrate disturbances via an unsupervised learning engine for dynamics. This capability leads to more precise maneuvers and an overall improved robustness of processes (McKinsey 2017a, p. 26). Digital Twins with 6D-simulation features enable us to reduce cycle times, to analyze material removal and to detect collisions.

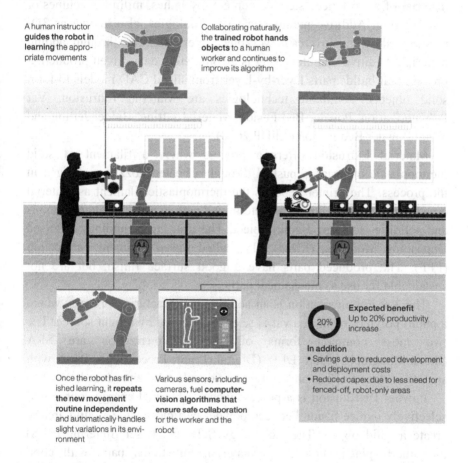

A human instructor **guides the robot in learning** the appropriate movements

Collaborating naturally, the **trained robot hands objects** to a human worker and continues to improve its algorithm

Once the robot has finished learning, it **repeats the new movement routine independently** and automatically handles slight variations in its environment

Various sensors, including cameras, fuel **computer-vision algorithms that ensure safe collaboration** for the worker and the robot

Expected benefit
20% Up to 20% productivity increase

In addition
• Savings due to reduced development and deployment costs
• Reduced capex due to less need for fenced-off, robot-only areas

Fig. 2.12. Collaborative and Context-Aware Robots (McKinsey 2017a, p. 27).

Robotic Process Automation (RPA), smart workflows and artificial-intelligence techniques such as machine learning, natural language tools and cognitive agents will improve efficiency, eliminate errors and reduce operational risk (Berruti *et al.* 2018, p. 2).

2.1.3.4 *3D-Additive Manufacturing (AM)*

Additive manufacturing opens up a new perspective in manufacturing and has the potential to become a new key technology. Traditional production technologies are subtractive technologies, reducing the material of a workpiece step by step e.g. by lathes, milling machines or laser cutting. Additive manufacturing technologies, also known as 3D-printing, allow us to create workpieces very flexibly through adding material. Additive manufacturing is a completely data-driven production process that builds parts layer-by-layer from sliced CAD models to form solid objects. Available technologies are Material Extrusion, Vat Polymerization, Powder Bed Fusion, Material Jetting, Binder Jetting and Metal Powder Bed Fusion (AllDP 2018).

Material Extrusion offers a process where a filament of solid thermoplastic material is pushed through a heated nozzle, melting it in the process. The printer deposits the thermoplastic filament as material on a build platform along a predetermined path, where the filament cools and solidifies to form a solid object. The printing technology is Fused Deposition Modeling (FDM), also called Fused Filament Fabrication (FFF). The produced parts have a good surface finish, but are not sustainable for use as mechanical parts.

The Vat Polymerization is an additive manufacturing process, where a photo-polymer resin in a vat is selectively cured by a light source. The two most common forms of Vat Polymerization are SLA (Stereolithography) and DLP (Digital Light Processing). Parts with smooth surface finishes and fine feature details can be produced.

Powder Bed Fusion is a process where a thermal energy source will selectively induce fusion between powder particles inside a build area to create a solid object. The technology Selective Laser Sintering (SLS) uses thermoplastic powder as material. Functional parts with good mechanical properties can be produced.

Material Jetting is a manufacturing process where droplets of material are selectively deposited and cured on a build plate. Photopolymers or wax droplets that cure when exposed to light can be used. The printing technologies known as Material Jetting (MJ) and Drop on Demand (DOD) use photopolymer resin as material. Material Jetting (MJ) works in a similar way to a standard inkjet printer, but the print head jets hundreds of tiny droplets of photopolymer and then cures/solidifies them using an ultraviolet (UV) light. Drop on Demand (DOD) uses a pair of ink jets. One deposits the build materials, the other is used for dissolvable support material.

Binder Jetting is an additive manufacturing process where a liquid bonding agent selectively binds regions of a powder bed. Binder Jetting (BJ) can be performed with sand or metal powder, such as stainless steel or bronze, as material. It can build objects of large volume and even functional metal parts at a low cost.

Fig. 2.13. 3D-Printed Turbine Blades (Siemens 2018g).

Metal Powder Bed Fusion is a process which produces solid objects, using a thermal source to induce fusion between metal powder particles one layer at a time. The associated technologies are Direct Metal Laser Sintering (DMLS), Selective Laser Melting (SLM) and Electron Beam Melting (EBM). These are using metal powder made from aluminum, stainless steel and titanium as materials. DMLS heats powder to a point at which it can fuse together on a molecular level. SLM uses a laser to achieve a full melt of the metal powder so that it forms a homogeneous part. Electron Beam Melting (EBM) uses a high energy beam, or electrons, to induce fusion between the particles of metal powder. These technologies can be applied for strong, functional parts with complex geometries (AllDP 2018).

With these advanced technologies, it is already possible to produce complex high-tech items such as blades for turbines (Fig. 2.13), or a burner head in gas turbines (Siemens 2018h).

Additive manufacturing offers the unique advantage of creating prototypes and specific products in more flexible, efficient and economical ways. The component geometry of innovative products can be adjusted or scaled up or down without any need for tool changes. Physical inventories can be replaced with digital inventories, which allows us to reimagine products, reinvent manufacturing and rethink business. The vision of digitally transforming the global manufacturing industry and accelerating the delivery of reimagined parts made with industrial additive manufacturing is moving into reality. Additive Manufacturing tools for engineering, simulation, product preparation and machining are merged in integrated systems and offer the possibility of achieving a rapid transition when scaling up from prototyping and small-series production on single machines to fully industrialized series production (Siemens 2018h).

The full disruptive potential of additive manufacturing will unfold if there is direct access to highly valuable services. Seamless collaboration and integration between designers, manufacturers and technology providers is required. Manufacturing systems and crucial knowledge for engineers, designers and machine operators have to be available globally. Additive manufacturing networks and collaborative additive manufacturing platforms make knowledge and technology accessible to the market with the aim of facilitating innovative parts and creating high-performing additive manufacturing production cells within a smart enterprise. On-demand design and engineering expertise, knowledge, digital tools and production capacity for additive manufacturing can be made available through global networks. This allows us to create completely new business models, such as online collaboration facilitating digital transactions that source high-quality parts (Siemens 2018i). Industrial 3D printing is moving from being a technology used for rapid prototyping to an additive manufacturing technology used for serial production. Additive manufacturing facilitates the optimization of supply networks and the production of highly innovative components. In future additive manufacturing will become a key enabler for disruptive components and end-to-end digital production.

2.1.3.5 *Human Work and Resource Planning*

In digital enterprises, workplace environments can be analyzed with virtual models of humans. The designs and operations for a wide variety of human factors, such as injury risk, timing, user comfort, reachability, line-of-sight, energy expenditure, fatigue limits and other important parameters can be investigated. The goal is to improve compliance with ergonomic standards during all product design and manufacturing engineering stages. Human work can be organized efficiently in order to enhance workplace safety and efficiency and rework can be avoided by uncovering human performance and feasibility issues early.

Human resource planning, performed in a collaborative, data-managed 3D simulation environment, enables realistic simulation of human tasks. Human resource simulation has the goal to improve workplace ergonomics, in order to increase productivity and to raise the motivation of workers on the shop floor with better workplace conditions. The deployment of cognitive tools leads human workers to focus on higher value activities, industrial quality, consistency and auditability in business processes. Human workers can use these techniques to interface with robots in more human related ways, providing the opportunity for humans and machines to interact and cooperate seamlessly, driving new levels of efficiency and productivity (Williams and Allen 2017, p. 4).

2.1.4 *Manufacturing Operations Management (MOM)*

Manufacturing Operations Management focuses on the operation of industrial enterprise systems and offers an operational view of the enterprise. Manufacturing Operations Management as an evolution of the Manufacturing Execution System (MES) is designed to digitalize production processes into an integrated management system, including advanced planning and scheduling, asset management, compliance management, manufacturing execution, performance analysis and quality management. This includes product and production tracking to communicate real-time manufacturing data automatically from the shop floor and gives a real-time view of the production processes and environment. Product and production tracking offer data from several sources. This data can be analyzed from different perspectives, such as by product, work in process, route, tools, equipment, material and labor.

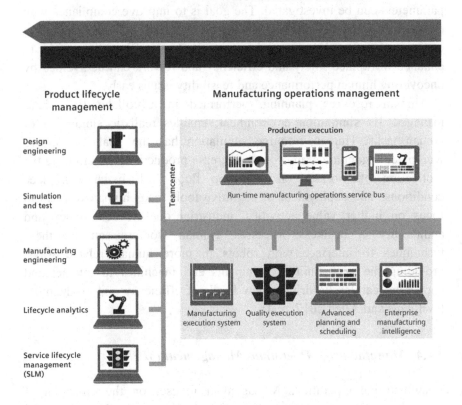

Fig. 2.14. MOM Enterprise Platform Approach (Siemens PLM Software 2018, p. 14).

MOM and PLM are accessing partly the same issues, PLM from a product-related perspective and MOM from an operational-related point of view. In the operational phase of all modelling and simulation activities, we have to consider that the results of these activities are required in nearly real-time in order to improve the actual system. MOM offers a holistic approach which provides full visibility into manufacturing processes to steadily improve manufacturing operations performance. Also, MOM enables us to implement strategies for the complete digitalization of manufacturing operations focusing on improved efficiency, flexibility and time-to-market. The availability of real-time data improves the digitalization and integration of the operational part of the production. MOM integrates, connects and unifies data sources such as the Manufacturing Execution System (MES), the Quality Management System (QMS), Advanced Planning and Scheduling (APS), Enterprise Resource Management (ERP) and others into accessible analytical data models providing us with the capability to explore and drill down into contextualized data (Siemens 2017a).

The operational management in digital enterprise environments can improve responsiveness, flexibility and agility by synchronizing materials, resources and assets. Best practices across the enterprise and supply operations can be identified in order to operate lean, to improve order fulfillment and to minimize waste and to reduce unplanned down time. The lead time and inventory shall be reduced and the control and synchronization across manufacturing operations shall be improved. The response to unplanned events across supply networks accelerates the capturing of information to drive continuous improvement and prevention programs (Dassault Systèmes 2014 p. 4). Through interfacing the factory floor level by real-time process monitoring and control with the management level, Manufacturing Operations Management captures operational knowledge, increases efficiency and improves agility.

2.1.4.1 *Routing, Sequencing and Dynamic Balancing*

Operative production planning requires the routing, sequencing and scheduling of orders to production resources. Allocating orders to the factory floor on single, parallel or multiple lines, as well as splitting and merging lines, requires advanced planning strategies and detailed information from the factory floor. Flexibility in modern enterprise systems requires us to route and schedule many different products and variations with small lot sizes to be produced through a complex production environment in order to meet the customer demand. Simulation and Artificial Intelligence-based approaches can assist us to improve and optimize routing and scheduling quality.

The mechanism of pull processes, triggered by actual events instead of forecasts, is the base of many successful manufacturing strategies, such as Make-to-Order (MTO) and Just-in-Time (JIT). Pull processes are the key to enable efficient customization and to compensate for forecast errors as events occur.

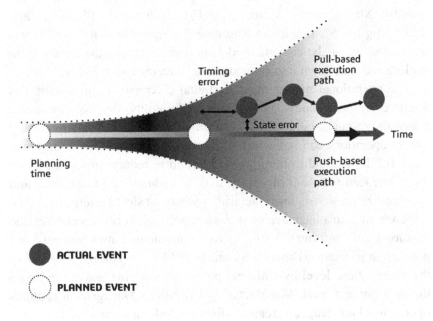

Fig. 2.15. Pull Approach (Dassault Systèmes 2017b, p. 4).

Smart-Pull manufacturing provides a combination of pull-based business processes, actionable operational intelligence and informed corrections to achieve better business performance and to take mass customization to new levels. Three major types of mass customization based on pull can be applied. The collaborative pull mechanism has the ability to draw out people and resources inside and outside of an enterprise to collaboratively design a solution that addresses needs as they appear. Its enablers are virtual prototyping, simulation, additive manufacturing or networking and enterprise search. Through IIoT intelligent sensors, cloud computing and network platforms, Manufacturing-as-a-Service (MaaS) can be carried out on-demand.

Adaptive pull is the most common type of pull used in manufacturing and logistics operations. Within traditional Lean Manufacturing, pull-based processes are being powered by digital technologies to eliminate over-production and inventory (Dassault Systèmes 2017b, pp. 4-5). For all pull processes, an efficient operational model is required for sensing, controlling and synchronizing resources to execute pull mechanisms.

Load balancing requires us to consider the operating cycle times of all particular production and logistic modules in the production environment. This is done to generate the corresponding processes for all resources involved, in order to balance the load. Discrete event simulation models combined with robotic or machine simulation can provide a dynamic perspective of some part of the production environment or even the complete production environment. Dynamic load balancing is required to analyze actual throughput based on real-time data, work-in-process, resource utilization, buffer sizes and utilization in order to improve production systems.

2.1.4.2 *Digital Supply Networks (DSN)*

Digital disruption will change supply mechanisms in digital enterprises from linear supply chains to supply networks. This shift from linear, sequential supply chain operations — design, plan, source, make and deliver — to the interconnected, open systems of Digital Supply Networks (DSNs) will change the way enterprises compete in future (Mussomeli 2016, p. 2). To avoid becoming a victim of disruption, it helps to understand these shifts and adapt accordingly. Supply networks integrate information from many different sources and locations to drive the physical acts of production and distribution in order to enable integrated views of the supply network.

In Digital Supply Networks there is potential for interaction between each node and every other point of the network, allowing for better connectivity among areas (Fig. 2.16).

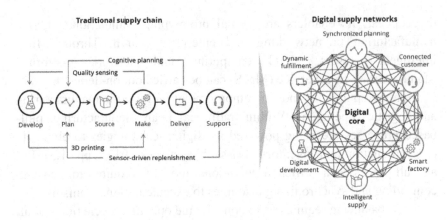

Fig. 2.16. From Supply Chains to Digital Supply Networks (Mussomeli *et al.* 2016, p. 6).

Communication is multidirectional, creating connectivity in what traditionally has been disconnected by links in the supply chain. This transition from linear to network structures requires us to open a new way of linking physical and digital assets. The main characteristics of the DSN are always-on agility, connected community, end-to-end transparency, holistic decision making and intelligent optimization to enable broader strategic transformations. Instead of planning incremental improvements within a supply chain, the supply network can be used to fuel growth across the business (Mussomeli *et al.* 2016, p. 8).

2.1.5 *Totally Integrated Automation (TIA)*

Interfacing the controls on the factory floor with the planning and operational levels, Totally Integrated Automation offers real potential throughout the entire value chain. TIA enables seamless interoperability between automation technologies and horizontal and vertical data integration from the field to the management level. Real-time interfaces between devices on the factory floor and high-level enterprise systems are mandatory for digital enterprises. IIoT-technology enables us to transform automation inside highly automated factories. Sensors across the factory floor are gathering information and businesses will be able to feed this information back through machine learning algorithms to identify trends that forecast future outcomes. Communication that requires enormous computing power and improvements in robotics, machine learning and Artificial Intelligence are leading us into a new automation phase. This allows us to optimize the automation processes with real-time-data, enhanced decision making and feedback into the automation level to ensure continuous optimization. As the requirements and available technologies are changing, the methods of automation and consequently the nature of human work are changing also (Lowes *et al.* 2017, p. 4).

Digital advances, better interfaces and the use of Artificial Intelligence will enhance operations and the performance of production and logistic systems. The IIoT-technology and big data analytics will lead to more automation in digital enterprises. Integrated production and robot systems in advanced production networks can perform a range of physical work activities better and cheaper than humans, including activities which required cognitive capabilities once considered too difficult to automate successfully. Advanced analytics and totally integrated automation will improve productivity, efficiency and effectiveness and also have an impact on employment and productivity in the global economy.

2.1.5.1 *Interfacing Physical and Digital World*

For interfacing the digital world with the physical world, sensor systems are absolutely essential. Sensor systems enable us to monitor and analyze multiple machine variables to improve performance, reliability and energy efficiency. Sensors can deliver vital insights into machine state and health. With modern sensor technology it is possible to affordably collect in a single piece of equipment large amounts of data from multiple sensors, to analyze that data in real time and to detect upcoming problems before these actually happen.

For the efficient use of data, it is very important to acquire data of good quantity, quality and reliability and to receive these data at the right time. If the data are not available in time, the actual processes cannot be improved and these data can be used then for statistical evaluations only. For operational purposes real-time data are mandatory.

Fig. 2.17. Interfacing the Physical World (Siemens 2018g).

It is important to know the time span taken for data acquisition, including data preprocessing and data transfer to the computer device, where decisions based on these data have to be performed. The admissible timespan available for real-time data depends on the dynamic of the analyzed processes and devices.

Sensor technology is moving from single sensors towards integrated sensor systems in IIoT-frameworks. The performance of sensor systems has increased significantly and at the same time the cost of sensors, network hardware, computing power, data storage and communication bandwidth have fallen dramatically. Standard interfaces and modern integrated electronic hard- and software have made powerful sensor applications cheaper and faster to implement at scale. Wireless communication, handhelds and wearable devices have made access easier. The performance of data analysis, even data analysis already integrated in sensor systems, has improved and is moving towards Artificial Intelligence techniques (Schuh *et al.* 2017).

However, the high number of sensors will increase the number of network connections and the amount of traffic and data in an enterprise.

Therefore, in terms of traffic, smart sensor systems shall integrate advanced preprocessing and analytic possibilities locally at the edge and shall send a minimum of data through the network. These short bursts of data may be sent frequently or infrequently. Larger amounts of data may have to be sent depending on the use case and the actual traffic of the network.

2.1.5.2 *Automation Decisions*

Automation decisions must align with business and operations strategy and have to show a clear return on investment. Automation can achieve objectives such as reducing costs and improving quality, flexibility and worker safety. Automation strategies require decisions on multiple levels regarding technologies and the level of automation. The right balance for any enterprise will depend on its overall strategy, its business goals and its enterprise culture. For each automation decision it is important to start with a clear definition of the problem. For each project it is important to identify where and how automation can offer improvements to the enterprise strategy. And automation has of course had an impact on the actual situation of human work places.

Fig. 2.18. Automation Decision (Siemens 2018g).

To maximize flexibility and economies of scale in automation strategies, modern approaches for production systems request platforming and modularization strategies which simplify and reduce the cost of managing complex product portfolios. Process platforms can be standardized, applied and reused in multiple applications. This simplifies programming, maintenance and product support. Automation systems and modules will need to be highly integrated into enterprise systems, requiring new technology and also changes in management processes, culture and mind-sets (Tilley 2017, p. 72).

With the use of modern integrated automation portals, it is possible to apply engineering frameworks including a range of practical digitalization functions to shorten engineering times through standardization and engineering efficiency. TIA Portals enable teamwork and enhanced diagnostics of machines and systems including real-time monitoring and advanced analysis. The inclusion of multifunctional platform controllers enables high-level applications to be created and reused with technical and commercial programming tools in a TIA Portal. This includes the integration of kinematic handling functions into controllers, interfacing and programming robots. Controls and robot technologies are growing closely together including advanced drive systems (Siemens 2017c).

2.1.6 *Total Quality Management (TQM)*

In industrial enterprises there is a demand for high production quality and reliability to fulfill customer delivery demands. Yield losses have to be kept small and costs in the planed limit. In digital enterprise approaches modern machine learning is capable of handling visual inspection and quality assurance to increasingly improve quality. These systems are able to abstract from differences in illumination, imperfect surface orientation, or the presence of irregular background textures and focuses on defects only (McKinsey 2017a, p. 30).

AI engines have learned to detect even in complex manufacturing environments the particular products which need to be reworked due to defects. A typical application of AI-based quality testing in automotive industries is shown in Fig. 2.19. Another typical use case is a semiconductor chip production process, where cycle times from the first processing of the wafer to the final chip typically require several weeks and include various intermediate quality-testing processes (McKinsey 2017a, p. 28).

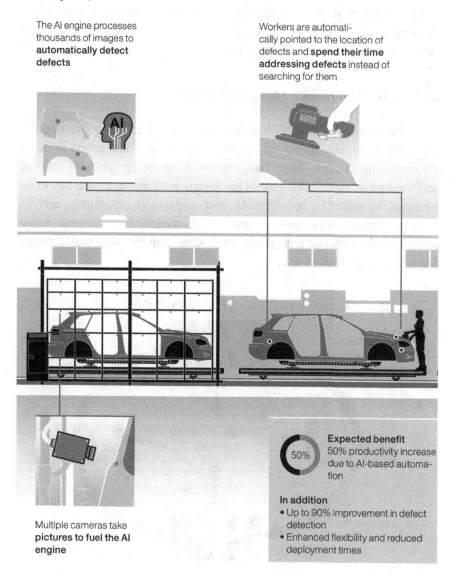

The AI engine processes thousands of images to **automatically detect defects**

Workers are automatically pointed to the location of defects and **spend their time addressing defects** instead of searching for them

Multiple cameras take **pictures to fuel the AI engine**

Expected benefit
50% productivity increase due to AI-based automation

In addition
• Up to 90% improvement in defect detection
• Enhanced flexibility and reduced deployment times

50%

Fig. 2.19. Automated Quality Testing (McKinsey 2017a, p. 31).

With the use of Artificial Intelligence, the product operating and processes can be optimized to significantly reduce defects. To enhance yield, AI-based analytics with supervised and unsupervised machine-learning systems can be applied to predict the locations of yield detractors (McKinsey 2017a, p. 28).

2.1.7 *Asset Performance Management (APM)*

Asset Performance Management has the goal of enabling the optimal asset reliability, availability and performance of physical assets in order to make operations safer and more reliable to ensure optimal performance at sustainable cost. The operation of an enterprise has to be managed in order to reduce risks and unplanned downtimes and to decrease maintenance costs. Asset Performance Management using connected devices and data analytics is changing the way maintenance can be conducted nowadays.

Fig. 2.20. Essential Components of APM (Bailey 2018).

Modern enterprise assets are equipped with a high variety of sensor systems, which are producing large amounts of real-time-data. IIoT-technology allows us to connect these data through local and global networks in order to optimize Asset Performance Management in digital enterprises towards Predictive Maintenance (PM). Proactive and predictive maintenance enables us to act before costly failures occur.

Intelligent asset strategies balance the competing priorities of reducing cost, improving availability and reliability and managing risk to optimize overall asset and operational performance even across multiple sites. Implementing an effective APM strategy requires integrated, connected enterprise solutions that enable asset-intensive organizations to drive safer, more reliable operations, while facilitating optimal performance at sustainable cost (Bailey 2018).

Asset Performance Management (Fig. 2.20) requires us to provide a unified view of the asset state at any time and anywhere, using advanced analytics and digital twin models to predict equipment failures before these occur. The goal is to ensure compliance with expanding regulatory requirements. With maintenance strategies it is important to continuously collect and manage data for each asset in order to learn from continuous, real-time analysis and therefore to understand the options for avoiding potential problems while balancing associated costs, risks and benefits to make the best business decisions that help to maximize operational performance (Bailey 2018).

A predictive use case of mechanical production system maintenance (Fig. 2.21) shows AI-enhanced predictive maintenance using powerful analytics and cloud technologies in order to enable predictive maintenance with smart decisions based on cognitive analysis and insights. Predictive maintenance drives improved asset utilization and reduces maintenance costs as well as improved product quality and availability.

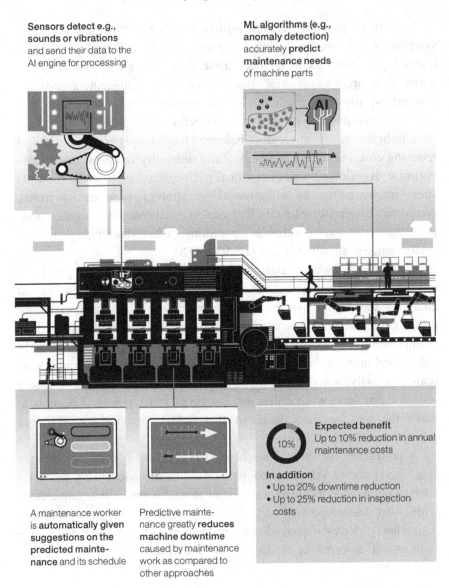

Fig. 2.21. AI-enhanced Predictive Maintenance (McKinsey 2017a, p. 25).

2.2 Enterprise Models

Modern digital enterprises require a holistic approach with new and flexible digital strategies to optimize the entire value chain (Deloitte 2018a). These digitally-driven enterprises require enterprise models on various levels for the planning and operation of the systems control. The models have to consider the integration of product lifecycle management, manufacturing operations management, electronic design automation, application lifecycle management and more.

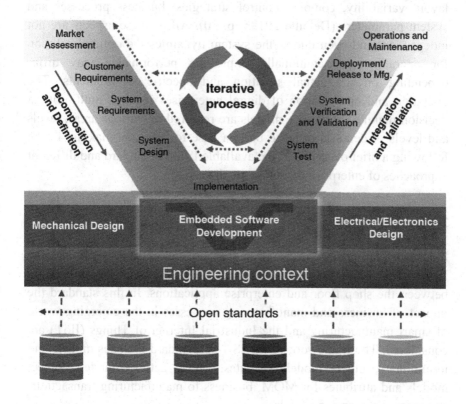

Fig. 2.22. Enterprise Engineering Aspects (Mayer 2017).

Through the use of integrated software solutions, a digital image of the entire value chain can be created (Cotteleer and Sniderman 2017). These digital enterprise platforms have to offer an integrated portfolio of automation technologies and software-based systems for industries to seamlessly integrate and digitalize the entire value chain. With Digital Twin concepts, virtual clowns of the value chain can be created (Parrott and Warshaw 2017, p. 7). These digital clones allow us to simulate, to test and to optimize in a completely virtual environment in order to increase efficiency, flexibility and quality and to reduce time to market. The Digital Twin concept enables optimization in the virtual world and the subsequent transfer of results to the physical world.

Production and logistic enterprises are complex systems, in terms of layout variability, complex control strategies, business processes and system parameters (Deloitte 2018b, p. 20). All of these aspects are not independent and even due to the system dynamics the optimal solution for operating and continually improving performance may differ depending on the actual situation and specific requirements. The operation and optimization of digital enterprises requires multi-criteria decision-making. Enterprise models are required on various areas, levels and levels of detail in order to build a base for decision making. In the following a brief overview of the available ISA-95 standard and different approaches of enterprise modeling are discussed.

2.2.1 *ISA-95 Standard*

Industrial enterprises can be structured on hierarchical levels and the ISA-95/IEC 62264 standard has been established for the integration between the shop floor and enterprise applications. In this standard the impact of business and manufacturing processes in the emerging world of smart manufacturing and the Industrial Internet of Things (IIoT) are considered. The framework of the ISA-95 standard includes models and terminology, object model attributes, MOM activity models, object models and attributes for MOM, business to manufacturing transactions and messaging service models.

The ISA-95 standard uses a clear hierarchical enterprise model with five levels (Fig. 2.23). Level 0 describes the actual production and logistic process. Level 1 defines the sensing and basic control of the actual processes. Level 2 encompasses monitoring and automated control systems. Level 3 covers activities in the areas of production and logistics operation management, quality management, maintenance and inventory management. Level 4 corresponds to strategic and tactical enterprise management with activities in the areas of business planning, purchasing, sales, long-term planning, management of enterprise locations, logistics and human resources (Fig. 2.24). Each level in the model is a dedicated component in the information architecture and always has to integrate with the levels above and below.

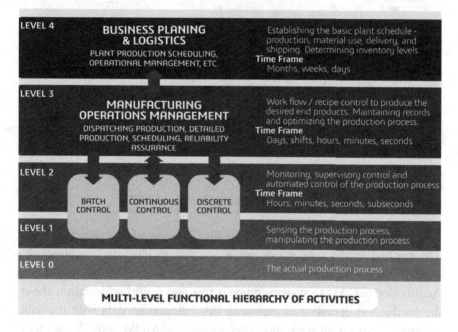

Fig. 2.23. ISA-95 Systems Hierarchy Model (Dassault Systèmes 2017c, p. 3).

The Manufacturing Operations Management (level 3), is based on the production levels 1 and 2 and consists of operations activities such as scheduling, tracking, performance analyses, etc. A generic activity model has been defined to represent production control, quality, maintenance and inventory operations for manufacturing including information flows between functional areas within a production capacity and flows from those areas up into the enterprise (Adams *et al.* 2007).

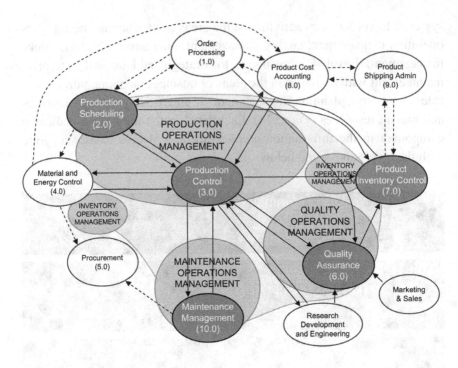

Fig. 2.24. ISA-95 Functional Enterprise Model (Adams *et al.* 2007).

The information flow between the level 4 enterprise system and level 3 is applied to the four major areas, such as production, maintenance, quality and inventory (Fig. 2.25). Supervisory Control and Data Acquisition (SCADA) systems convert this into useful information about the production operation. Combining this automation data with the data captured from employees and other processes, MOM provides a more complete, real-time view of multiple plants and the supply chain, including planning and scheduling (Dassault Systèmes 2017c, p. 5).

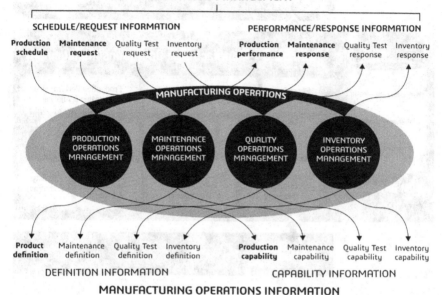

Fig. 2.25. ISA-95 Manufacturing Operations Information (Dassault Systèmes 2017c, p. 5).

2.2.2 *Monolithic Enterprise Systems*

Monolithic Manufacturing Operations Management Systems are software solutions that include most ISA-95 functionality in one software system. Monolithic MOM systems are mostly running in one plant and are usually managed through a specific database in the plant. The usability in distributed environments is often limited (Hughes 2017, p. 13).

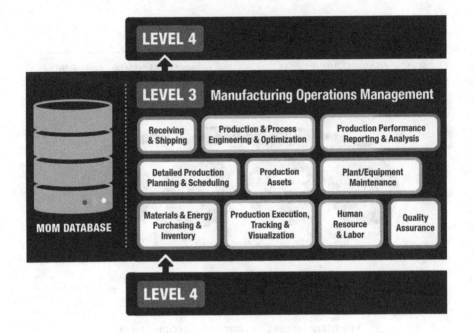

Fig. 2.26. Example for a Monolithic MOM System (Hughes 2017, p. 13).

Many Industrial Enterprises have already had monolithic MOM systems in use for some years, doing a good job. Through the integration with IIoT the requirements are changing and these platforms have increasingly been replaced by modern, distributed modular approaches on IIoT Platforms or MOM Apps (Hughes 2017, p. 15, 17).

2.2.3 *Distributed Enterprise Modular Systems*

Modular MOM will move into IIoT or Cloud platforms. Going modular involves choosing an IIoT based solution and many of these have rich functionality and a strong installed base (Fig. 2.27). Due to the demands of flexibility and IIoT integration, distributed modular MOM systems offer an approach to modularize existing MOM solutions to make it easier to transition to new IIoT platforms (Hughes 2017, p. 15).

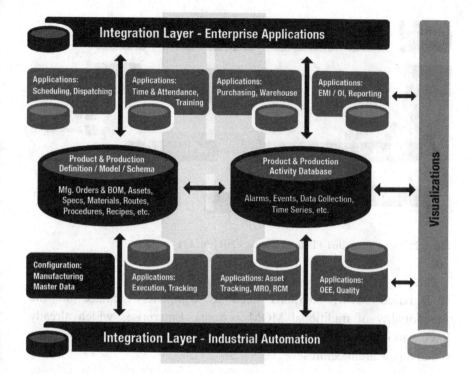

Fig. 2.27. Traditional Database-Centric Architectures (Hughes 2017, p. 15).

2.2.4 *Apps on an IIoT Platform*

IIoT platforms will enable us to move all types of functionality, including MOM, to the IIoT. A consequent advanced approach is to offer the complete MOM functionality as Apps on IIoT Platforms (Fig. 2.28). This approach offers the best connectivity and flexibility for future demands. These Apps can be the starting point for plant integration and further optimization.

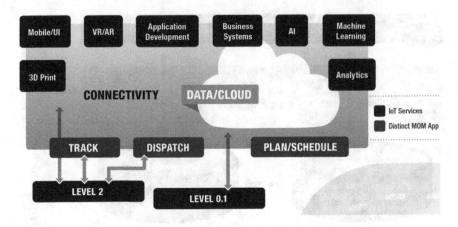

Fig. 2.28. Apps on an IIoT Platform (Hughes 2017, p. 17).

However, existing systems have a comprehensive functionality and IIoT based MOM solutions need to completely replace all the functionality of traditional MOM systems. Enterprises which already have a monolithic MOM system in use need to bridge the gap between old and new architectures.

2.2.5 *Closed Loop Approach*

Modern software solutions shall provide closed-loop approaches for continuous improvement. The closed loop tightens the alignment of the virtual world with the physical world in a continuous, iterative process. Closed-loop approaches enable us to synchronize and optimize products and production across design, planning, manufacturing execution, automation and service. A collaborative, connected information loop can be created in order to improve the manufacturing process to accelerate the delivery of products at the optimal level of time quality and costs.

Regarding production, the focus of the loop is on synchronizing the highly efficient production of the current product. The focus of closed-loop quality is on improving the quality of the product across the entire product lifecycle. The purpose is to ensure the quality of the current product and feed quality information back into the production and design processes to improve the quality of the next-generation products.

For closed loop manufacturing the collaboration backbone is required, which carries the digital thread to seamlessly integrate all solutions of a digital enterprise. Product lifecycle management is the key to convert ideas to products faster and MOM is the real-time layer that links PLM to automation, connecting the virtual world of product development with the physical world of production (Siemens PLM Software 2018, p. 10).

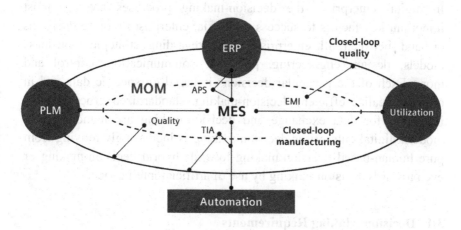

Fig. 2.29. Closed-loop Manufacturing (Siemens PLM Software 2018, p. 14).

At the heart of closed-loop manufacturing the MOM portfolio is used to integrate all the other parts of the technology infrastructure to create the intended product for the user. The MES is used to connect all parts of the production process and to integrate all the other parts of the value and innovation chain. Advanced planning and scheduling (APS) translates demands into production planning. TIA, as the interface to the smart machines and Electronic Manufacturing Intelligence (EMI), delivers data for performance and quality management. Quality is an important part of the system. This ensures the quality of the product being manufactured. It also moves a cross lifecycle quality process into a larger closed loop (Siemens PLM Software 2018, p. 14).

Chapter 3

Enterprise Decision-Making

In digital enterprises the decision-making processes are the most important key factors to success. Industrial enterprises require decisions on and between all enterprise levels regarding strategies, business models, design, engineering, planning, communication, control and more. Each of the particular decisions is based on specific data and in order to realize efficient decision-making, standardized processes and interfaces for data exchange and decision-making are mandatory. In modern digital enterprises decision-making is increasingly moving from pure human-based decision-making towards hybrid decision-making or even towards decision-making by use of artificial intelligence.

3.1 Decision-Making Requirements

Due to the complex dynamic of digital enterprise systems in terms of layout variability, complex control strategies, business processes and system parameters, the decision-making process is not trivial. Processes and parameters are not independent and the optimal solution for the same requirement may even differ depending on the state of the actual system dynamics. Decision-making processes require us to classify, define and specify the answer to the problem, deciding what is right rather than what is acceptable. In practice, decision-making has to meet boundary conditions and the validity and effectiveness of the action to be carried out has to be tested. These steps are the basis of the decision-making process to enable effective decisions to be carried out in time (Ducker:1967wd).

Some important aspects of decision-making are speed and adaptability, accuracy and consistency, reliability and transparency of decisions. Speed and adaptability are critical capabilities, especially when a real-time response is required. Predictive analytics enables forecasts and projections to be more accurate and precise, when the right data is provided. And accuracy is of special importance when the consequences of small deviations are high. Consistency and reliability are important to ensure the quality of the decisions made. And transparency allows for decisions to be reviewed and improved upon in the future. When two parties in a transaction have different sets of information, this may lead to suboptimal decision-making and a lack of acceptance of the decision made.

As organizations become more agile, the improvement of decision-making can be accelerated through categorizing the type of decision to be made and tailoring the approach accordingly.

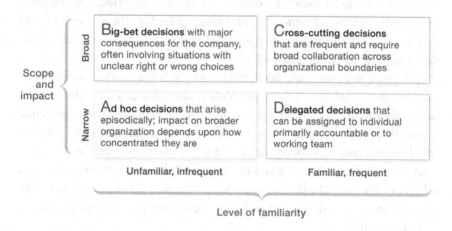

Fig. 3.1. ABCD of Decision-Making (De Smet, Lackey, *et al.* 2018, p. 3).

Big-bet decisions are infrequent and high-risk decisions, which have the potential to shape the future of an enterprise. Cross-cutting decisions are frequent and high-risk decisions, which are a series of small, interconnected decisions made by different groups as part of a collaborative, end-to-end decision process. Delegated decisions are frequent and low-risk decisions, which can be effectively handled by an individual or a working team, with limited input from others. And *ad hoc* decisions are infrequent, low-stakes decisions without major impact (De Smet, Lackey, *et al.* 2018, p. 3).

In digital enterprise systems, subsystems and devices always interact in an interrelated environment. Decision-making to improve the operational behavior of enterprise systems requires us to understand the interrelationship and interaction between subsystems and devices. The operation and system optimization of industrial enterprises needs data and simulation-driven multi-criteria and multi-actor decision-making approaches on all levels. Decision-making in digital enterprises has to be performed in decision phases (horizontal axis) and decision levels (vertical axis).

3.1.1 *Decision Phases - Horizontal Integration*

Decision-making in industrial enterprises can be classified into the three horizontal phases of strategic planning, planning the processes and systems and operating the processes and systems. Related to each phase, the requirements for decision-making vary.

Strategic decisions are concerned with business models, changes of the organizational structure or production structure and size, the general production technology and related production equipment, the principal layout of production and logistic systems and the general configuration of planning and control systems. Strategic decisions are made for a relatively long time horizon and the data available for decision-making is relatively limited. On the strategic level the goal of decisions is not to provide an extended level of technical detail but to guide us towards a certain direction.

In the planning phase, decision-making deals with establishing or changing processes and systems. Production and logistic processes have to be planned and the related system resources allocated. Decisions on this level are limited by the direction and boundary conditions given by the guiding decisions on the strategic level.

Operational decision-making has to deal with the actual operation of the existing enterprise systems. These decisions are typically concerned with issues such as production scheduling, routing, lot sizing, sequencing and setting priorities for production and logistic jobs. Operative decisions are made for a relatively short time horizon. The availability of data is high and decisions have to be made fast and very much in detail. However, decision-making on this level is limited by the preconditions given by the decisions from the planning and strategic level.

3.1.2 *Decision Levels - Vertical Integration*

Industrial enterprises require decisions regarding design, engineering, planning, communication and controls on different enterprise levels. Decisions in digital enterprises have also to cover various hierarchical levels (Fig. 3.2), from single devices or components of machines on the factory level, to production cells, up to decisions on the top management level of an enterprise.

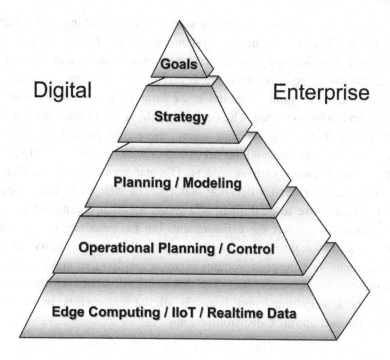

Fig. 3.2. Digital Enterprise Decision Pyramid.

Each of the particular decisions requires specific data, models and algorithms. On the factory floor there are large amounts of data from connected IIoT devices available and decisions have to be performed due to the demand being nearly in real-time. On the top level, strategic decisions with guiding impact on the long run have to be performed. For the vertical integration in digital enterprises a meaningful information exchange between these levels is mandatory. Digital enterprises have to use standard data interfaces between the applications on different modelling levels in order to enable collaboration with virtual models for different purposes and levels of detail (Dassault Systèmes 2017c). Open architecture, open interfaces and interoperability are key factors for the successful integration of decision-making.

3.1.3 *Multi Criteria / Multi-Actor Decision-making*

One has to consider many criteria when decision-making in industrial enterprises. For a production system multiple criteria have to be optimized: the flexibility to adapt to customer requirements has to be increased, the costs have to be minimized, the throughput time of the products has to be minimized and at the same time the utilization of the system has to be increased. The decision-making has to take into account that all of these aspects and many more are important and not independent. Decision-making in multi-criteria systems is always a compromise between various aspects. The management has to decide on the strategic priorities for decision-making. The weights of these aspects and priorities have to be defined in a target function. Technical systems can efficiently support the management, but the priorities for decision-making and weighting the strategies are the responsibility of the management. In enterprise systems many actors have to make decisions and these influence each other. The communication between the various actors is a very important issue in digital enterprises in order to streamline and optimize decision-making.

3.2 Decision-Making Approaches

In industrial enterprises, decisions have to be made in time, with the required accuracy, consistency, reliability and transparency. Transparency allows decisions to be reviewed and improved upon in the future (Henke *et al.* 2016, p. 75). The requirements for decision-making are speed, availability, accuracy, consistency, reliability and transparency. For decision-making in digital enterprises, the speed and availability of the decision-making process is very important. Especially for decisions on the operational level of production systems, real-time or nearly real-time response is needed. If the decision-making process is too slow, the result may be useless.

Analytical algorithms based on real-time data can react very fast and improve the speed of decision-making. Accuracy is of special importance when the consequences of small deviations are high. Predictive models provided with the required data can give a clear view into future developments, leading to more effective use of resources. Consistency and reliability are very important for decisions to be accepted. Transparency allows for decisions to be reviewed and improved upon in the future. When the parties involved in a transaction have different sets of information, this can lead to suboptimal decision-making. With good transparency even difficult decisions are much better accepted by all parties involved (Henke *et al.* 2016, p. 75).

For decision-making, various approaches are available. The future trend of decision-making is moving increasingly from pure human decision-making towards algorithm-based decision-making, simulation-based decision-making and decision-making by use of artificial intelligence.

3.2.1 *Human Decision-making*

Classically, decision-making in enterprises is performed by humans and the advantage of human decision-making is the flexibility of the human brain in combination with the availability of human education, experience and creativity. However, human biases and heuristics are predominant in decision-making and data overflow or physical limitations may lead to decision mistakes.

Humans use imagination to create things in their minds before building them in the physical world and humans use ideas and concepts to inspire other people to co-create ideas and turn them into reality. The human imagination exists in the human virtual world. However, ideas created from the imagination can inspire large groups of other humans. Teams or larger groups of people can co-create a new reality. The domain of co-creation is almost limitless, especially when used in conjunction with elements of cyber physical systems such as Big Data Analytics and AI. This process is limited by imagination and perhaps by the laws of physics that will pose boundaries (Dijkstra and Smith 2018).

3.2.2 *Algorithm-Based Decision-Making*

Algorithm-based decision-making is based on clearly defined algorithms and can be performed by human or machines as well. The decision algorithms are defined by experts using knowledge from various sources, such as physics, mathematics or empiric experience for the particular use case. The algorithms can be defined as decision rules for humans or be implemented in software. Algorithm-based decision-making software allows us to use a large amount of data, which is processed in order to find the best possible decision based on the implemented rules.

A typical example of rule-based decision-making is the sequencing and routing of production jobs through the factory floor. In complex production and logistic enterprises with a high number of different products and processes, it must frequently be decided how jobs shall be scheduled and routed through the facilities in order to fulfil the required goals at a maximum. These decisions can be generated by a rule-based scheduling and routing strategy. A particular strategy can be built up from several priority classes, filtering and sorting rules that are defined as default rules in order to optimize the global system or at least to improve local requirements. Examples of such rules are that of Critical Ratio (select the job with the least time to due date divided by total remaining processing time), Shortest Setup Time (select the job with the shortest setup time), Critical Path (select the job on the critical path) or

Priority (select jobs with a special demand to be processed very urgently).

Rules can be used as a single rule or as a network of combined rules in order to consider different aspects and create priorities adapted to the use case. In the past, rule-based decision-making has brought significant productivity improvements to enterprise software. However, because modern enterprises are very complex and due to the dynamics of the systems, the effects of rules are very difficult to oversee. Therefore, in the course of daily business, production planners mostly use only a few of the available sets for the daily operation of the company. Nowadays simulation technology offers a powerful approach to test various strategies and modifications without disturbing the current production.

The quality of algorithm-based decision-making depends on the quality of the defined rules and it can be as flexible as the algorithms are formulated. Rule-based decision software is limited to the implemented algorithms and cannot learn and improve with experience as humans can. System changes may require a change of algorithms to be adapted to the new situation by an expert again. With modern AI-technology more advanced approaches will be possible.

3.2.3 *Simulation-Based Decision-Making*

Simulation can answer what-if questions by use of simulation models and simulation runs without affecting the physical system. In a simulation cycle (Fig. 3.3), a model (Digital Twin) is built from the physical system by abstracting the relevant functionality of the physical system. This model is used to perform experiments answering what-if questions. The gained insights are used to change the physical system or process.

Through simulation, technology decision-making can be supported on many enterprise phases and levels. Simulation technology allows us to test decisions using a model in the planning phase, in the realization phase or during the operation of the enterprise system. Increasingly, it is required not only to optimize a particular aspect of a system, but also to optimize systems from a global perspective, considering the interrelationship between the different aspects of a system, such as technology, administration, human resources and ecological impacts.

Simulation-based decision-making offers the possibility of improving decision-making for the layout planning, the production logistics, the robotic planning and more.

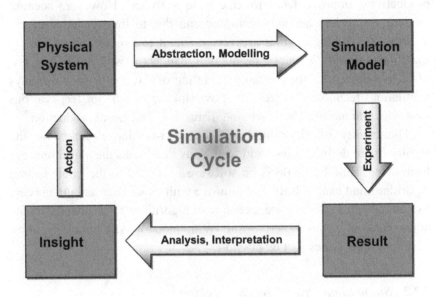

Fig. 3.3. Simulation Cycle.

Typical applications of simulation-based decision-making in industries are discrete-event simulation for the planning of new, or the changing of existing, production and logistic systems. 3D-motion simulation focuses on the layout, optimization and programming of robot systems. By use of simulation the planning quality can be improved and structural and administrative changes can be tested.

For each planning level, different types of decision-making are suitable (Fig. 3.4). On the level of devices and components, a detailed simulation model can be used for investigating mechanical or electrical components. Kinematics simulation can be used to plan and program the motion of single machines or production cells, such as robot applications.

Logistic simulation is used for analyzing time related interactions in production cells, production areas or an entire factory.

The structuring of simulation at different hierarchical levels allows us to build comprehensible models and to cope with particular requirements at each particular level. Through this structure, the results of a simulation which deals with the details of an assembly process can be used on the next level to plan and program the robot motion in the particular assembly cell with the use of a kinematics simulation. On the next level, some results may be used in a logistic simulator to plan the information and material flow of a production area consisting of several machining and assembly cells. Above the level of simulating a complete factory, a next level of simulation can deal with the interrelationships between factories and enterprises. Simulation studies in the planning phase, which test and evaluate the planning of production, logistic and robotic systems, have been state of the art since more than 20 years ago.

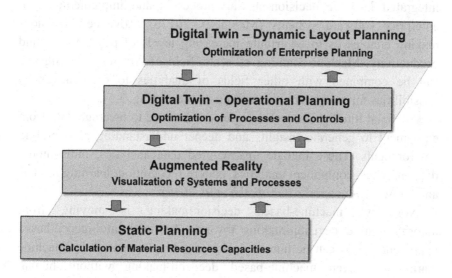

Fig. 3.4. Enterprise Planning and Control Levels.

Due to IIoT, real-time interfaces and increasing computational power, simulation is not limited to the planning phase. When decision-making is used to improve the operational production and logistic processes, it is focused on the operational production and logistic controls, such as control strategies, scheduling or routing of orders. Simulation in this phase has to be performed in nearly real-time and requires real-time data. The result of this simulation is required immediately so that it can be used for the immediate improvement of the operational system. The simulation models for this operational phase have to be updated automatically on the basis of real-time data at any time and the results have to be fed back to the operational system immediately in nearly real-time.

3.2.4 *Artificial Intelligence-Based Decision-making*

Decision-making can be improved significantly by the use of Artificial Intelligence technologies (McKinsey 2017b). Due to advances in computer processing power, nowadays machine learning can be integrated into the decision-making processes and implemented into enterprise software systems (McKinsey 2017b). Advanced decision-making enables us to contribute increasing levels of performance and productivity. Machine learning as a sub-field of Artificial Intelligence can be combined with other fields of analytics to offer advanced possibilities for many decision-making use cases (Fig. 3.5).

Artificial Intelligence technologies can be used to leverage data from equipment to generate insights and deeper understanding of operating environments. These include unstructured data analytics, multi-modal data analytics, component analytics, pattern recognition, learning models and knowledge networks (Gramatke *et al.* 2017).

Nowadays machine-based decision-making is moving from algorithm-based decision-making towards Artificial Intelligence-based approaches. This can be human decision-making supported by machine learning or even machine-based decision-making without human interaction. An example of how Artificial Intelligence and neural networks can optimize complex systems is a Siemens gas turbine. Even after experts had done their best to optimize the nitrous oxide emissions from the turbine, the AI system was able to reduce emissions by an additional ten to fifteen percent (Siemens 2018b).

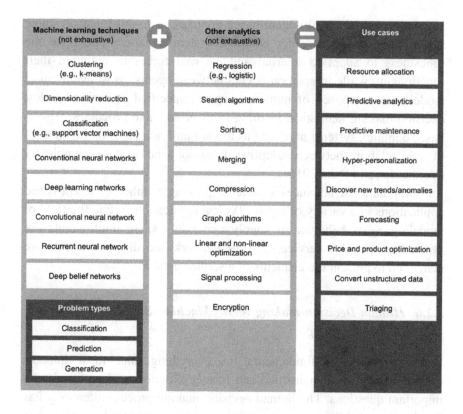

Fig. 3.5. Machine Learning and Analytics (Henke *et al.* 2016, p. 12).

3.2.5 *Agent-Based Decision-making*

Multi-agent-based approaches, as the actions and interactions of autonomous agents, can be used to service decision-making. A negotiation mechanism among the agents is required in multi-agent based simulation models to map their dynamic characteristics in a service delivery context. Agent-based modeling and simulation is a relatively new approach to modeling systems comprised of autonomous, interacting agents. Agent-based decision-making uses dynamic networks of many interacting agents. Each agent has a distinct state transition and processing mechanism which can be highly coincident with the actual situation owing to the flexibility and operability of multi-agent based simulation models. Multi-agent-based approaches do not focus on stable states. The models consider complex system dynamics and have the robustness to adapt to internal and external forces to maintain their functionality while interaction occurs between agents. Most agent-based models are composed of numerous agents specified at various scales, decision-making heuristics, learning rules or adaptive processes. Agent-based complex systems may lead us toward unifying algorithmic theories of the relation between adaptive behavior and system complexity (Vermeulen and Pyka 2016).

Computational advances enable a growing number of agent-based applications in a variety of fields. Typical applications are in the field of modeling agent behavior in supply networks, where multi-agents are utilized to model a service delivery network and different agents are generated to present the elements of a service network.

3.2.6 *Human Decision-making versus Machine-Based Decision-making*

Decision-making is fundamental to everything, and most humans ultimately rely on their instinct and former experience when faced with important questions. The human decision-making process often only has a subject probability of success, is sometimes not really clear, or is limited by the human inability to process information overload. Algorithms can support humans in decision-making through the use of data and analytics. With the use of data and analytics, we can bring in more data points, break down information and add automated algorithms to improve the decision-making process. While humans sometimes experience information overload, automated algorithms can weigh a big amount of data. Automated algorithms and decision-support tools can help to avoid errors that have serious consequences. Increasingly there are more data from various sources available and the data grow richer and more diverse. This opens up the possibility of using the resulting insights to make decisions faster, more accurate, more consistent and more transparent (Henke *et al.* 2016, p. 11).

Data and analytics can turn decision-making into a more data-driven approach, helping us to avoid human limitations and biases. Analytics can help to overcome human limitations to improve speed, accuracy, consistency and transparency of decision-making (Henke *et al.* 2016, p. 75). Machines and algorithms are generally predictable and reliable, do not tire or miss data points and draw on the same information without varying their conclusions each time.

Depending on the scale and complexity of the decision-making problem, we choose to use either manual, rule-based or machine-learning-based decision-making (Fig 3.6). Humans have imagination, ideas, inspiration and cognitive abilities. Human limitations in decision-making can be partly overcome through the use of data and analytics. Digitalization can support human decision-making by offering data, the results of data analysis and the calculation of decision algorithms. Today there is a flood of data from many sources, such as IoT sensors and other digital interfaces. While humans can experience information overload, automated algorithms can weigh a large amount of data and help us to avoid problems that have serious consequences with the use of decision-support tools (Henke *et al.* 2016, p. 75).

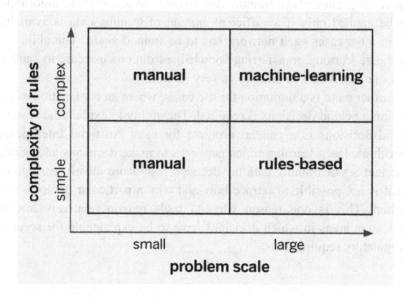

Fig. 3.6. Decision-Making (Wellers *et al.* 2017, p. 9).

Cyber-physical systems focus on sensing and using AI technologies such as Deep Learning and Knowledge Graphs for decision-making (Dijkstra and Smith 2018). The possibilities of Artificial Intelligence have increased significantly during the last few years, but Artificial Intelligence is still narrow. A computer program could beat the human champion of the Chinese board game Go but without help the same computer would not be able to learn how to play chess, even though chess is significantly less complex than the game of Go (Deloitte 2017, p. 12). The most important advantage of human decision-making is still the flexibility and the capability that humans have to transfer knowledge and to find creative solutions.

3.2.7   *Reliability of Machine-Based Decision-Making*

The limitations of using machine-based decision-making are in the areas of data labeling, obtaining massive training data sets, explaining decisions and generalizing learning. Most machine-learning algorithms require large amounts of training data in order to learn. These algorithms can be applied only if a sufficient amount of training data is available and in most cases each network has to be trained again. The ability to generalize learning, transferring knowledge from one use case to another or from one network to another, is very limited.

Further there is a limitation for use cases, where an explanation of the reasoning behind decisions is required. The ability to explain the reasons behind decisions is a general problem for most Artificial Intelligence algorithms. Deep learning trains networks to make decisions and with a sufficient set of training data the decision results are mostly very good. But it is not possible to retrace how and why a particular decision was reached. This is one reason why AI tools remain relatively low in application areas in which decisions have to be explainable for security or regulatory requirements.

3.3 Digital Twins Concepts for Decision-making

The Digital Twins concept is a very powerful advanced concept for decision-making. Digital Twins (Fig. 3.7) are a virtual representation of physical objects or systems and offer an approach to improve decision-making through using real-time data and other sources to enable learning, reasoning and dynamic recalibrating for improved decision-making (Mikell and Clark 2018). The goal of Digital Twins is to monitor, simulate and improve equipment and processes in a virtual environment by bridging the physical and virtual worlds.

Digital Twins are virtual clones of real assets or processes. As the physical source changes, the data from the physical asset or process are collected in real-time and are replicated into a virtual equivalent in order to improve decision-making (General Electric 2016). A virtual copy of a system or process is created (Fig. 3.7) and this digital clone allows us to simulate, to test and to optimize in a completely virtual environment in order to increase efficiency, flexibility, quality and to reduce time to market. The Digital Twin concept enables optimization in the virtual world and the subsequent transfer of results to the real world. Digital Twins offer us the strong potential to achieve better insights into their objects and to drive better decisions to improve products and processes continuously (Shetty 2017).

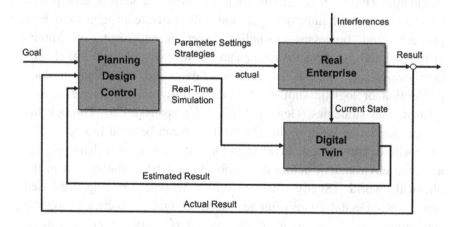

Fig. 3.7. Digital Twin as a Virtual Clone of Physical System.

The Digital Twin idea is not new. In the early days of space exploration, NASA was the first to experiment with a predecessor of a Digital Twin, called pairing technology (Oracle 2017). The principal concept of a Digital Twin had already been proposed in 1994 (Kuehn 1994) and the term "Digital Twin" had been introduced by Dr. Michael Grieves at the University of Michigan in 2001, who originally defined this in the context of Product Lifecycle Management (Grieves and Vickers 2001). The idea was to create digital records of serialized parts and raw materials to better manage recalls and warranty claims tracking requirements, to predict and detect quality trend defects sooner and to improve overall quality. System availability can be improved and asset-specific life managed through optimization and controls to reach a desired outage target, the reduction of unplanned outage, through continuous monitoring and prognostics. Warranty costs and services can be reduced and operational flexibility improved by creating more predictable, faster starts for flexible objectives. Product design and engineering can be improved in order to reduce operation costs, time to market for new products and lead time. In the end, all of these goals shall lead to revenue growth opportunities (Grieves 2014, p. 1).

With IIoT technology, the Digital Twins can be efficiently linked to real-world objects and offer information about how asset states respond to changes (Parris *et al.* 2016). In production and logistic enterprises, Digital Twins will improve operation and generate insights into how products and processes, including asset management, operational efficiency and maintenance repair can be improved (Oracle 2017). The monitoring and analysis of real-time data and advanced product, production or logistic simulation models allow us to improve design, controls and strategies (General Electric Company 2016). Through the use of simulation models, the Digital Twins can be used to operate the enterprise or parts of it in advance and to test drive several alternatives in a virtual environment before a decision is applied to the system in the physical world (Shetty 2017). With Artificial Intelligence-based capabilities, Digital Twins offer advanced product, production or logistic simulation models to optimize the system (Chistty 2017). A holistic

Digital Twin approach with continuous improvement will help us attain the best possible results (Siemens 2018f).

3.3.1 *Closed Loop Approach*

The core of the Digital Twin concept is a closed loop approach (physical-to-digital-to-virtual-to-physical). This closed loop approach starts with collecting data (physical-to-digital) then analyzing these data and decision-making (virtual) and giving feedback to the physical system or system control (virtual-to-physical) in order to change the physical system based on the gained insights. These steps can be repeated in a loop continuously in order to improve the system.

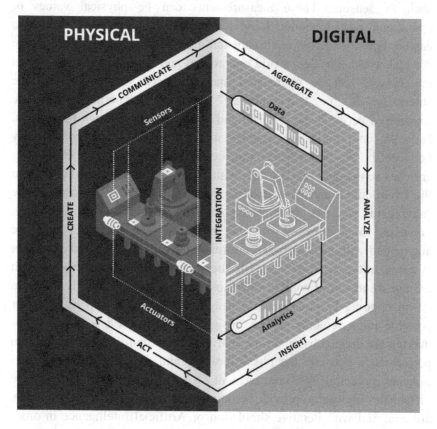

Fig. 3.8. Manufacturing Process Digital Twin Model (Parrott and Warshaw 2017).

The product, production or logistic model, based on real-time data, allows the monitoring and analysis of the assets to improve design, controls and strategies. With a simulation or Artificial Intelligence approach it is possible to head off possible problems before these can occur. This closed loop prevents delays and downtime, exposes new opportunities and even improves future planning. In general the Digital Twin approach (Fig. 3.8) contains an interaction of six steps, which completes the closed loop connection between the physical world and the virtual model of the Digital Twin (Cline 2017).

In the "create" step (1), various inputs from the physical process and its environment are measured by use of integrated smart components such as sensors. These measurements can be physical values or operational measurements. Sensors create signals that enable the twin to capture operational and environmental data from the physical process in the real world. Physical world operational and environmental data from the sensors can be aggregated and combined with data from the enterprise. In the "communicate" step (2), technology data are transferred between the physical and digital worlds through integration. Network communication enables a seamless real-time connectivity between the physical process and the digital platform. Edge processing enriches sensor and process data with business and contextual data from the environment and passes relevant data along to the platform. In the "aggregate" step (3), the real-time data are sent into a data repository, processed and prepared for the analytics. The measures may be augmented with process-based information from planning and execution systems. In the "analyze" step (4), the aggregated data are analyzed with the use of advanced analytics technologies, simulation and visualization on an ongoing basis to produce insights and identify opportunities for possible improvements. In the "insight" step (5), models for decision-making are created based on the analyzed data. Significant differences in performance between the physical world and the Digital Twin model indicate potential for improvement. Simple models visualize these differences in order to provide recommendations. More advanced models are analysed with iterative simulation or Artificial Intelligence in order to generate insights for decision-making. In the "act" step (6), the knowledge and recommendations from the "insight" step can be fed back to the physical world in order to transform the physical enterprise. The insights may feed into software systems on an operational level with actuators or even directly into actuators for movement and control or they may be subject to human intervention. With this interaction, Digital Twins complete a closed loop that modifies the physical world (Parrott and Warshaw 2017).

These six steps are easy to list. However, they require significant effort to achieve. Enterprises that embrace Digital Twins have the opportunity to better understand and continuously improve products, services and processes, which gives them a competitive advantage (Cline 2017).

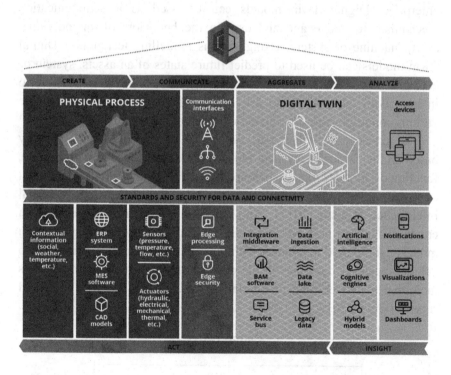

Fig. 3.9. Digital Twin Conceptual Architecture (Parrott and Warshaw 2017).

The Digital Twin conceptual architecture (Fig. 3.9) is based on these six steps. Digital Twin architectures can be built for multiple industrial levels and applications. Typical for all are the transfer of data from the physical asset to the virtual model and the feedback given that can alter the physical system. The particular virtual model can vary significantly based on demand, use case, technology available and modelling effort.

3.3.2 Digital Twin Types

The Digital Twin concept is very powerful and its typical benefits are visibility and the ability it gives us to understand and explain behaviors, predict behavior, perform what-if analysis and connect disparate systems such as backend business applications. Digital Twins allow visibility in the operations of an asset, an interconnected system or even a complete enterprise. Digital Twin models can be used as a communication mechanism to understand and explain the behaviors of an individual asset, machine or system. Using various modelling techniques, Digital Twin models can be used to predict future states of an assets, system or enterprise. As virtual models build on real-time data, it is possible to interact with the model and ask it what-if questions and to simulate various conditions that are impractical to create in the physical system.

The concept, structure and complexity of Digital Twins can vary based on the particular business objective and use case. There are simple, functional Digital Twins, which are based on clearly defined functional or parameter levels, and there are Digital Twins using Artificial Intelligence (Chistty 2017). An Artificial Intelligence algorithm can create insights to improve the asset, system or enterprise. Digital Twin models can be used to connect with the backend business applications to achieve business outcomes in the context of supply network operations including manufacturing, procurement, warehousing, logistics and field service (Oracle 2017, pp. 1-2).

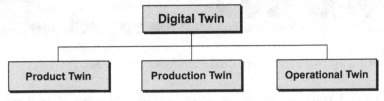

Fig. 3.10. Types of Digital Twins.

Digital Twins can be classified into three types — Product Twins, Production Twins and Operational Twins.

3.3.2.1 *Digital Twin of the Product*

Product Twins are created when a new product is defined and designed. This type of twin enables the visualization, simulation and validation of the products, including their mechanic, electrical or electronic functionality and the functionality of the product-related software.

Fig. 3.11. Product Twin (Siemens 2018).

With Production Twins, the quality of the product, the number of prototypes and the time-to-market of products can be substantially reduced. For marketing issues, Product Twins can be used in virtual show rooms, giving the customer an impression of the product. With Product Twins, customers can configure the product individually to their specific demands. Product twins can also be used as an input for defining the configuration, the layout and the engineering of the production systems in order to paralyze product and production development and to speed up time to market.

3.3.2.2 *Digital Twin of the Production Process*

Production Twins allow us to improve the planning, simulation and optimization of the production process. These Twins are virtual models of production assets used to predict the behavior and to optimize the performance of production systems. With the Production Twin the performance of production units can be predicted, bottleneck areas can be improved and it can be ensured that the products are produced according to what customers expect. Further Production Twins allow us to generate, test and validate the code for machine and robotic controls in advance. For smart production systems the use of Digital Twins as a verification/validation tool is essential.

Fig. 3.12. Production Twins (Siemens 2018).

3.3.2.3 *Digital Twin of the Operational Performance*

Operational Twins capture physical asset performance data from products and plants in operation. These Twins are constantly fed with real-time data from the product and the production facilities. Through the real-time connection with integrated automation components, the shop floor provides all relevant information. Data from smart connected products in the field and factory equipment are aggregated, analyzed and transformed into actionable information to create a completely closed loop decision environment for continuous optimization of the enterprise operation. This leads to new insights which can be fed back into the physical system via IIoT in order to establish a fully closed decision-making loop for the continuous optimization of the production process.

To reiterate, the Product Twins improve systems engineering, the Production Twins focus on manufacturing engineering and the Operational Twin enhance the operation of production and logistics. Together, they form a holistic approach to improving the manufacturing process. This combination creates a high-quality, agile and efficient manufacturing enterprise, transforming the operation into a more efficient one focusing on delivering innovation with speed and quality (Siemens PLM Software 2018, p. 8).

Digital Twins also include Virtual Twins, which virtualize devices by use of observed data, Predictive Twins, which build analytic models using a variety of techniques to suit the complexity of a problem and Twin Projections, which project insights generated by the twins back to the application with the use of IIoT.

3.3.3 *Digital Twin Modelling Levels*

Inside each Digital Twin, a conceptual architecture has to be designed for flexibility and scalability in terms of sensors and messages, applied analytics and processing in order to enable the creation of advanced architectures, which evolve rapidly with growing demands (Parrott and Warshaw 2017).

The models inside Digital Twins may be very different from each other, depending on the type of the twin, the specific use case and the required level of detail. The models allow us to predict in the virtual world how something would look, act or perform in the physical world, in order to gain insights. These models (Fig. 3.11) can be augmented reality models to visualize products or production devices, analytic algorithms analyzing data, simulation models to answer what-if questions or Artificial Intelligence models for advanced decision-making. All of these models are fed with data from the digital thread and require that tools and systems are able to communicate with each other.

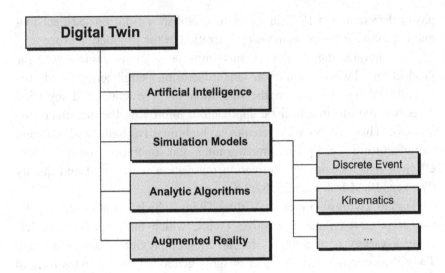

Fig. 3.13. Digital Twin Models.

3.3.4 *Augmented Reality Models (AR)*

On the first level, Digital Twin models can be augmented reality models. The data from the physical system are used for monitoring and improving transparency. Real-time visualization focuses on the visualization of the particular situation of an asset.

Augmented reality starts with a camera-equipped device such as a smartphone, a tablet or smart glasses equipped with AR software. When a user points the device at or looks at an object, the software recognizes this through computer vision technology. Based on this, the required information about the object is downloaded from the cloud. This information may be general information about the object, such as static 3D-data from a CAD System or actual real-time data from the object.

In a Digital Twin application, AR can provide a view partly of the real system and partly of the virtual model. This applies to products, assets or processes. Users can control these by touchscreen, voice or gesture. An operator can use an AR headset to interact with an industrial robot, to see superimposed data about the robot's performance and to gain access to the controls.

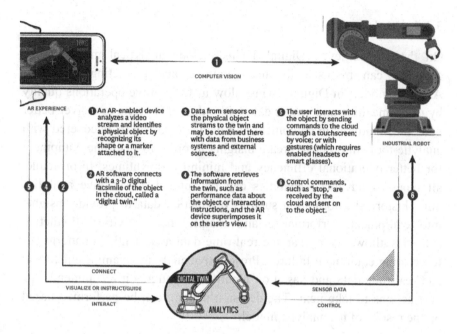

Fig. 3.14. Augmented Reality (Porter and Heppelmann 2017, p. 14).

As the user moves, the size and orientation of the AR display adjust to the shifting context automatically. New graphical or text information comes into view, while other information passes out of view. In industrial settings, users in different roles, such as machine operators or maintenance technicians, can look at the same object at the same time but be presented with different AR experiences that are tailored to their specific needs. The base for AR is usually a 3-D model, available in the cloud. This model has usually been created by use of CAD tools during the development phase, although it can also be established with the use of digitizing technology. The Digital Twin collects real-time information from an asset and also from external sources to reflect the current reality. It then creates a model in which the AR software accurately places and scales up-to-date information on the object (Porter and Heppelmann 2017, p. 14).

Augmented reality models inside Digital Twins do not support decision-making itself. These models are created so that human users can visualize the actual situation in order to improve their decision-making.

3.3.5 *Analytical Models*

On the second level, Digital Twins include analytical models. Data analytics can be used for understanding and predicting situations. Analytic models in Digital Twins allow us to improve operations quality by using machine and sensor data with other data assets to deliver better outcomes. Patterns in equipment and device data can be uncovered with analytic tools in order to create insights in order to fine-tune equipment for better operational efficiency and minimize downtimes. In principle, all types of advanced analytics can be applied. Descriptive analytics mine historical information such as production data to provide insights into equipment performance and maintenance activities. Predictive analytics allows us to examine real-time data and identifies patterns for forecasting equipment failures. Prescriptive analytics examines historical and real-time data and based on identifiable patterns it recommends the best actions to take next. The decision-making can be performed based on the results of the analytic model.

3.3.6 *Simulation Models*

On the third level, Digital Twins implement simulation models in order to answer what-if questions. Closed life-cycle data loops allow a prescriptive approach for decision support. This advanced Digital Twin approach uses simulation technology to improve decision-making. The simulation models implemented for Product, Production and Operational Twins differ regarding their type and level of detail.

For Product Twins, mainly 3D-Simulation models are applied in order to simulate the geometrical and mechanical system behavior of products, particularly with regard to assembly possibilities and other use cases. Additionally for mechatronic or electronic products, the functional simulation of the electronics and software is an important issue.

For Production Twins, several models can be applied on each level by use of hierarchical models. In robotics or NC-machining applications, kinematics simulation models dominate. In the fields of production and logistic flow, mainly discrete event simulation models are applied. Depending on the particular aims of each model, different levels of detail are required. For complex tasks in the digital enterprise it is advisable to define manageable subtasks and to model these separately, rather than using a single model for all purposes. For example, the motion paths and processes of robots in a complex production cell can be modelled and programmed by use of a detailed model, taking detailed motion control parameters and strategies into consideration. On the next level only selected results of this detailed model, such as handling times, may be used for the logistic model on the production flow level.

For Operational Twins, the requirements are different again due to the real-time demand for operational decision-making in a complex dynamic system. The simulation inside the Digital Twins has to be performed nearly in real-time. This requires a rapid and flexible modelling approach with lightweight simulation models. For lightweight models, the required geometry, characteristics and attributes are selected without the addition of unnecessary details. This reduces the size of the models and allows for faster processing. Light-weight models can simulate complex systems, including physical behaviors, in nearly real-time. The time and cost of communicating is substantially less and these models can be shared within the enterprise and throughout the network. Operational Twins enhance collaboration, understanding and the quality of product and process information.

In order that operational models can be generated nearly in real-time, the creation of the models can be performed by an automated model generation approach based on real-time data. The great advantage of this approach is that the model can be automatically generated from the current data and the state of the data and the simulation model always matches. If necessary, specific model details may be defined in greater detail by use of predefined specific building blocks.

3.3.7 *Artificial Intelligence Controls*

On the fourth level, more advanced Digital Twin models are using Artificial Intelligence technologies to leverage real-time-data, generating insights into and deeper understanding of operating environments. Artificial Intelligence can be used deductively for continuous improvement. The algorithms used may include unstructured data analytics, multi-modal data analytics, component analytics, pattern recognition, learning models or knowledge networks.

Artificial Intelligence and machine learning can analyze enormous amounts of data to reveal patterns and enable true predictability. Combining Digital Twins that use these technologies with powerful analytics tools allows us to predict trends. This will enable us to follow and monitor every component of a product or production process, from design through delivery and service. It will improve performance and increase return on investment. Algorithmic advances, the availability of real-time data and the tremendous increases in computing power are moving Artificial Intelligence models into Digital Twins for advanced dynamic estimation and decision making.

3.3.8 *The Value of Digital Twins*

The design and realization of Digital Twins requires a powerful combination of digital plus industrial strength including deep physics knowledge and engineering design knowledge. Also, advanced sensing and inspection technologies expertise, analytics experience and Artificial Intelligence is required. The potential business advantages of operational Digital Twins are advanced performance monitoring and the control and optimization of plant productivity regarding output and efficiency (Parrott and Warshaw 2017, p. 11; General Electric Company 2016, p. 11).

Digital twins are used to create business value along several axes by completing the knowledge loop from design and testing to production and operation and from data acquisition and analytics to improved service and then back again (Siemens 2018b). Digital Twins can be applied to individual assets in order to track history and performance over the lifetime of an asset. The Digital Twin infrastructure and models can be adapted to new scenarios or new factors. And advanced Digital Twin virtual models can be continuously updated as the physical asset is operated. An operational Digital Twin is at any time a faithful representation of the current state of the asset. In the sense of swarm intelligence, even hundreds or thousands of similar assets having a Digital Twin will allow the single asset to learn from similar assets (General Electric Company 2016, p. 7).

Operational Twin use cases will be in real-time or close to real-time. Using the Digital Twins can improve operational procedures and their use can even be embedded in the control system loop. Digital Twins in manufacturing will help us to detect potential quality issues earlier, or even improve the quality of the product being manufactured through the delivery of new insights. New revenue streams can also be created from the data itself. Digital Twins have initially focused on complex, high-cost assets, but increasingly the cost models for sensors, communication, analytics and simulation are decreasing. That will lead to the possibility of developing a Digital Twin of almost any product, production or logistic system (Wasserman 2017).

The precise economic value of Digital Twins will vary widely, depending on the economic models that drive the use case. Gartner predicts that by 2021, half of large industrial companies will use Digital Twins, resulting in those organizations gaining a 10% improvement in effectiveness (Chistty 2017, p. 2). To obtain the highest value from Digital Twins, the enterprise must address the digital ethics issues raised by different parties interacting with internal data and also the data from partners and customers. This will require enterprises to think about the value of the data and its contributions to the business and its partners and also to identify potential areas where the data could drive value but also pose risks (Chistty 2017).

3.4 Enterprise Optimization

Enterprise optimization requires decision-making on all enterprise levels and in all decision phases. In the mathematical sense optimizations lead always to an optimum, which is the best possible solution. Most of the aspects and parameters involved in an optimization are not independent and due to the actual situation the requirements for the optimization may differ significantly between cases. This makes optimization (Fig. 3.13) quite complicated. In digital enterprise systems the layout of manufacturing and logistics, the control strategies and a large variety of parameters have to be considered and optimized (Osan and Somers 2017). All these optimization and simulation topics are interconnected and changes in one topic always have an impact on the others. The optimization of a single topic can always lead to a sub-optimum only. Due to the complexity of the optimization of complex enterprises, multi-criteria decision approaches are required. Simulation technology can support decision-making on all phases and enterprise levels.

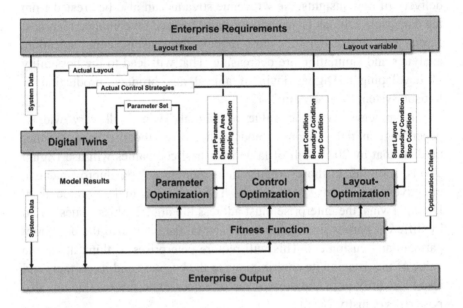

Fig. 3.15. Multi Level Optimization.

Due to time constraints and the complexity of industrial environments the term optimization is often also used for improvement, which means to find a good solution (80%) to improve the physical system in a short time but not to find an (100%) optimal solution after a long time.

3.4.1 *Mathematical Optimization / Improvement through Simulation*

Mathematical optimization models have the advantage that an optimum can be achieved directly by use of the mathematical algorithm. However, in the industrial praxis most systems to be optimized are very complex and have dynamic system behavior. In most of the use cases, it is not possible to define an appropriate mathematical algorithm for optimization which represents the system behavior sufficiently.

Compared to mathematical models, simulation models have the advantage of being applicable even for large and complex problems. Boundary conditions, even nonlinear conditions or failures, can be considered relatively easy in the simulation model. However, compared with mathematical models the disadvantage of simulation models is that these do not directly deliver an optimum. Each simulation run represents a single result und many of these simulation runs have to be performed in order to find a sufficient solution to an optimization problem. This approach provides a good solution, but it cannot be claimed that this solution is the global optimum.

3.4.2 *Agile Methodology*

Rapid changes in demands, market competition, technology and regulations make it more important than ever for enterprises to be able to respond and adapt flexibly and quickly (Ahlbaeck *et al.* 2017, p. 1). A new approach is required to bring about and lead an agile transformation successfully (De Smet, Lurie, *et al.* 2018, p. 1). The agile methodology approach reacts to these demands with the assumption that complex dynamic systems, such as digital enterprises, cannot sufficiently be controlled by rigid rules. Agile methodology has the ability to quickly and efficiently reconfigure strategies, structures and processes, people and technology toward an efficient solution. Agile organizations thus add velocity and adaptability to stability, creating a critical source of competitive advantage in volatile, uncertain, complex and ambiguous conditions (Aghina *et al.* 2017, p. 3).

Similar to living systems, agile organizations have to be stable and dynamic in order to survive in an unpredictable, rapidly changing environment, dealing with uncertainty and ambiguity with greater confidence. Innovative technologies and open nonhierarchical structures allow them to adapt flexibly to feedback, changes and demands (De Smet, Lurie, *et al.* 2018, p. 5).

To survive and enhance business, enterprises have to undertake a fundamental shift from a traditional organizational model to an agile model designed for the digital economy. This paradigm shift requires a new form of organization that enables innovation and collaboration at unprecedented speed, scale and impact. Agile organizations can develop products much faster, speed up decisions and reallocate resources (De Smet, Lurie, *et al.* 2018, p. 1). Agile control methodology requires software systems which are not based on rigid rules. These systems have to be built to react to any occurring change and disruptions very flexibly based on real-time data. This kind of software requires enhanced computing power, real-time interfaces and advanced information technology. With agile methodology automation is moving from linear waterfall approaches towards flexible approaches, where processes are broken into smaller components in order to perform analysis, development and testing in parallel.

Agile methodologies can drastically reduce risk in dynamic systems. The idea of agile control methodology is not to use virtual models outside of the system, but to make decisions directly on the fly and very flexibly according to the demands of the actual situation with the use of Artificial Intelligence. With the use of enhanced real-time data driven decision support, it is possible to reveal new opportunities for process improvement. Enterprise systems require the flexibility and agility to unlock these opportunities, and changes can occur within agile systems.

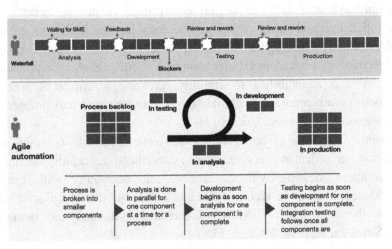

Fig. 3.16. Agile Automation Approach (Berruti *et al.* 2018, p. 4).

In agile enterprise systems products can be customized on the fly to meet specific consumer requirements and multiple products can use the same production lines in varied sequences without the need for manual tool changes. The speed of production lines can be adjusted to match changing customer demand. Rapid decisions and learning cycles can be applied by working in open networks of autonomous units and small, empowered teams based on a dynamic model that considers culture and leadership. Agile organizations always have to rethink the underlying technologies to support quick iterations, higher deployment velocity and flexibility through new practices and tools (De Smet, Lurie, *et al.* 2018, p. 6). Organizational agility requires practices such as shared vision and purpose. Actionable strategic guidance by use of sensing and seizing opportunities allows flexible resource allocation based on action-oriented decision architecture in flexible multi-purpose accountable cells including active partnerships and ecosystem in open physical and virtual environments. Agile automation at scale requires standardized ways of working, performance orientation, rapid iteration and experimentation (Ahlbaeck *et al.* 2017, pp. 14-16).

Information Technology for Digital Enterprises

For industrial enterprises, dedicated information technology is required, and due to the improvement of information technology during the last few years, modern concepts of digital enterprises are coming increasingly into practice. Therefore, the aspects of information technology which are important for digital enterprises are discussed in this chapter.

4.1 IT-Requirements for Digital Enterprises

During the last few years information technology has changed the world dramatically. In the private sector modern devices such as mobiles, tablets, wearables and the Internet of Things (IoT) have already had a huge impact and in the industrial sector the Industrial Internet of Things (IIoT) is growing fast. Fast and reliable manufacturing of individual products and the need to meet tight delivery schedules requires real-time communication and an extremely agile response. Increasing the digitalization of production processes requires openness, robustness, determinism and flexibility in industrial communication.

For commercial and especially industrial use, security is very important and the IT requirements for digital enterprises differ significantly from the IT requirements for private use. Some very important issues in the commercial and industrial sector are interoperability, system integration speed, real-time communication and security with increasing digitalization. The separation of commercial IT systems and industrial control systems has to be replaced by open, end-to-end networking that permits flexible, deterministic production.

4.2 IT Architecture

IT architectures are moving towards cloud computing, edge computing, platform-as-a-service or software-as-a-service. When they are implemented together, cloud computing is used to create service-oriented models and edge computing offers a delivery at the edge that allows for the execution of disconnected aspects of cloud service.

4.2.1 *Cloud Computing*

Cloud computing is the delivery of computing services by use of networking software, servers and storage, databases and analytics and more over the Internet. The cloud is a network of remote servers that are hooked together and meant to operate as a single ecosystem. These servers are designed to either store and manage data, run applications, or deliver content or services. A cloud can be a private, public or hybrid cloud. In a private cloud, technologies specific to the cloud model are hosted in an on-premises datacenter. The public cloud is defined as a computing service offered by a third-party provider over the public internet available to anyone for use or purchase. Public clouds are managed and maintained by large technology vendors offering access to storage, software and computing, available anywhere and anytime on a rental basis. A hybrid cloud is a computing environment that combines public and private clouds by sharing data and applications between these.

Cloud computing technology is ideal for IIoT applications due to its inherent flexibility, low starting costs and scalability. It is possible to start small and expand quickly, just like many IIoT projects do, with minimal upfront costs. The cloud offers the scalability and the flexibility to support a wide range of IIoT and big data projects without investment in local hard- and software. The user can start small and scale up quickly as data volume grows and more resources are required. When combined with big data technologies, massive amounts of IIoT data can be analyzed quickly while they are streaming into the cloud (Oracle 2016a).

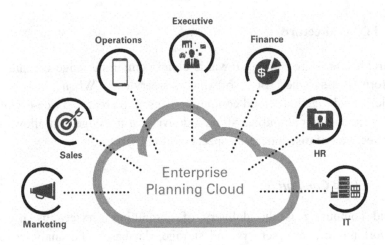

Fig. 4.1. Enterprise Planning Cloud (Oracle 2016b).

Cloud-based platforms give virtually any user the tools and storage capacity to conduct advanced analytics. Cloud-based storage and analytics services enable even small enterprises to store data and processes on distributed servers. Companies can purchase as much space as actually is required, greatly simplifying the data architecture and IT requirements and lowering capital investment. As computation capacity and data storage can be outsourced, many tools are becoming accessible and data can be more easily combined across sources (Henke *et al.* 2016). However, cloud computing is not free of charge. The user has to pay on demand and the transformation to cloud computing requires some effort. There are business, financial and a broad range of technology issues to be faced. When formulating the business strategy for cloud adoption, it has to be decided which workloads shall be moved to the public or private cloud. A hybrid cloud offers the best of both worlds. With a consistent cloud platform, enterprises can confidently make technology decisions based on business requirements, rather than business decisions based on technology complications (Microsoft 2018, p. 12).

4.2.2 *Edge Computing*

Edge computing refers to a computing infrastructure close to the sources of data. The edge is where the IIoT assets act, sensors gather data and actuators change machine configurations and behavior by responding to incoming commands. Significant improvements in performance can be achieved by processing or analyzing data within or near the assets themselves in real time. Gateways at the edge collect, filter and aggregate data, analyze these, and transmit the data to or from the network by translating protocols and providing a network security boundary.

Edge computing is a distributed computing paradigm in which computational power is shifted nearer to distributed device nodes. Applications logic pushes data and computing services from centralized servers to the edge of the network in order to come closer to the source of the action where distributed system technology interacts with the physical world. In the context of the Industrial Internet of Things, edge computing is where software meets physical devices (General Electric 2018a). Edge computing uses a similarly distributed systems architecture as centralized clouds but does so directly at the edge. The idea is to provide data analysis and Artificial Intelligence closer to the data collection sources and cyber-physical systems such as smart sensors and actuators to speed up computing and to reduce network traffic.

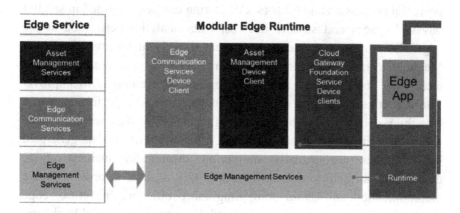

Fig. 4.2. Edge Computing (Siemens 2017d, p. 14).

Edge computing does not need a connection to a centralized cloud. However, the combination of edge computing and central cloud services offers very powerful applications. Edge Computing enables analytics and knowledge generation at the logical extremes of a network and covers a wide range of technologies including wireless sensor networks, mobile data acquisition, mobile signature analysis, cooperative distributed peer-to-peer ad hoc networking and processing. It is also known as local cloud, fog computing, grid or mesh computing. Edge computing includes distributed data storage and retrieval, autonomic self- healing networks, virtual cloudlets, remote cloud services, augmented reality and more (General Electric 2018a).

The use of modern edge devices provides advanced analytics in proximity to the equipment in a secure way. It will enable multiple use cases for descriptive, diagnostic, predictive and prescriptive analytics by leveraging cloud connectivity in combination with edge applications in an integrated hard- and software environment. A modern edge approach consists of modular edge runtime applications and cloud-based edge services, which need to synchronize from an engineering and runtime perspective. This edge approach offers a transparent integration of cloud services with field automation platforms enabling the seamless extensibility of an installed device base and edge applications at the field level (Siemens 2017d, p. 14).

The rise of edge computing is driven by less expensive and more powerful processors and sensors. Computing can be performed in smaller physical spaces and smaller devices. Data analytics performed at the edge allow us to generate improvement directly at the machine level. Machine learning, deep learning, neural networks and other advanced techniques for analyzing and understanding data continue to improve. Through edge computing significant improvements in performance can be achieved in real time by processing or analyzing data within or near the assets themselves. GE believes that roughly 3% of the data generated by machines are actually delivering meaningful insights. Edge computing can help to unlock the other 97% of data, in order to make communication and cloud computing more efficient. In future, edge computing will take increasing industrial computational workloads and in collaboration with cloud computing this is a perfect match (General Electric 2018a).

4.2.3 *Software- / Platform-as-a-Service (SaaS)*

Software-as-a-Service and Platform-as-a-Service are delivery models where functionality is hosted by a third party, rather than being installed on local IT infrastructure. Cloud computing which delivers on-demand computing applications is synonymous with Software-as-a-Service. The platforms, including hardware, networking facilities, software and data, are managed by the vendor. In a Platform-as-a-Service (PaaS) approach the applications and data are still managed by the client. In the Software-as-a-Service (SaaS) approach everything is hosted.

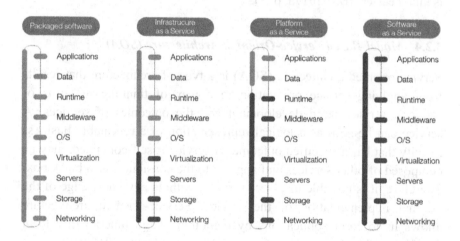

Fig. 4.3. Cloud Service Comparison (IBM 2017a, p. 4).

To offer Software-as-a-Service to customers instead of selling software to customers offers significant advantages. SaaS is typically paid for on a subscription or pay-per-use basis. The advantage for the customer is that in an early project phase the customer does not have to invest in soft- and hardware. It is possible to use the software on demand without buying the software. Through scalability the numbers of seats can be easily adapted to the actual needs of increasing or decreasing demands.

With a cloud-managed infrastructure, companies take advantage of the affordable and infinitely scalable computing capacity, which can readily accommodate the demands of global and fully digitalized enterprises. The platform can automatically scale to required data volumes and the numbers of connected assets and the number of users can be flexibly adapted on-demand by following a pay-per-use pricing model. However, in the long run this model might be even costlier for a customer using the software intensively. SaaS is more flexible than traditional deployed software. Software offered as a service has the advantage of always being up to date. The clients can always benefit from the latest functionality and for the supplier maintenance and support is much easier (IBM 2017a, p. 3).

4.2.4 *Model-Based Service-Oriented Architecture (SOA)*

Service-oriented architecture (SOA) is a type of architecture that results from applying service orientation to a way of thinking in terms of services, service-based development and the outcomes of services. A service can be seen as a logical representation of a repeatable business activity that has a specified outcome. A service is self-contained, may be composed of other services and appears to the consumers as a black box. Therefore, it is possible to access services without any knowledge of the internal implementation of the service. Service-oriented architecture allows us to form applications by combining large functionality from existing services in an *ad hoc* manner (The Open Group 2018).

Model-Based Service Oriented Architecture enables the rapid implementation of solutions either from scratch or starting with defined industry templates, thus driving significantly faster enterprise deployments. The forms, workflows, relationships structures and data model can be tailored and configured in real-time at a business level. In digital enterprises this service orientation can be used to consistently deliver sustainable business value with increased agility and cost effectiveness in line with changing business needs.

4.3 Internet of Things (IoT)

The Internet of Things enables communication between a huge number of devices with the use of a wide range of IoT technology. The approach offers unprecedented connectivity, automated data collection and data exchange between connected devices, such as machines, physical objects, vehicles or buildings embedded with sensors and actuators. The devices and products developed are more innovative, more data-centric, more interactive, continuously learning and they involve more software than ever. In a list of disruptive technologies, only the Internet of Things, the mobile internet, the automation of knowledge work, cloud technology and advanced robotics will have substantial economic impact (Menard 2018, p. 33) Similar to the rise of network technology in the 1980s and the rise of open source in the late 1990s, the rise of IoT will ultimately cause the streamlining and standardization of data exchange. The IoT is growing rapidly and in future all IoT devices will automatically and reliably connect to the best network or mobile network, based on location, usage, subscription and roaming agreements. Operations stay flexible without compromising security (Gerber 2017, p. 7). The IoT is not limited to improving and speeding up existing decision-making processes but it supports a new level of decision-making by providing enterprises with insights into situations that had never been observable before.

4.4 Industrial Internet of Things (IIoT)

The Industrial Internet of Things (IIoT), as the next step of the Internet of Things (IoT), is related to the real-time and security demands of industrial use cases. The IIoT has the potential to fundamentally shift communication and interaction in nearly all industrial areas. IIoT systems with sensors and actuators which are connected by networks to software can monitor and manage connected objects, such as machines and all kind of devices. This rapidly advancing technology makes it possible to apply data-driven decision making. From monitoring machines on the factory floor to tracking the progress of logistics and sensing changes in physical environments IIoT systems can enable companies to get far more benefit from their physical assets. This will revolutionize the running of enterprises. The value of IIoT technology is shifting from hardware and connectivity to software and analytics that make use of the data (Alsén *et al.* 2017).

For digital enterprises it is important to identify the three phases of IIoT deployment, each delivering increasing levels of value. The first is connecting devices and assets to gather data, enabling remote monitoring and the use of big data and analytics for business-level validation. In the second phase real-time and predictive analytics and machine learning can be applied to detect notifiable events from the high volumes of data enabling proactive decision making and driving improvements in product quality and service levels. On the third level service excellence is achieved by fully integrating IIoT data into enterprise processes and applications offering new products and services with a differentiated customer experience (Turner 2016).

IIoT technologies offer digital tools and improvements that support operations, communication, analysis and decision-making in modern enterprises across the four dimensions: connectivity, speed, accessibility and anchoring. Connectivity will change enterprise systems through the use of connected real-time data from sensors monitoring the entire production and logistic processes. Connectivity will support advanced analytical techniques and advanced decision making by use of actual stored data. Speed in comprehensive, real-time data collection and analysis is necessary for enterprises to become increasingly more responsive and to identify performance gaps. Accessibility of current and historical data by use of secure and tightly controlled interfaces is the key to improving, simplifying and accelerating the operation of enterprise systems (Gupta 2017, pp. 34-35).

The use of IIoT achieves an anchoring effect which improves enterprise communication and allows enterprises to collaborate more effectively. Barriers between functions can be cut down to ensure that decision-making reflects the interests of the business as a whole. Digital devices can create transparency between operational performance and profitability. Due to an LNS Research study the top use cases of the IIoT will be remote monitoring (28%), energy efficiency (27%), asset reliability (25%), business model transformation (24%), production visibility (22%), quality improvement (22%), asset and material tracking (17%), internet enabled products (15%) and others (LNS Research 2018, p. 6). The Industrial Internet is the key to a modern industrial business strategy and is growing at twice the rate of the consumer Internet (General Electric 2018b).

4.4.1 *Requirements for Industrial Communication*

The requirements for industrial communication differ from those for private or commercial communication. Safe and fast connectivity is the foundation of the Industrial Internet, especially when timing is critical and every millisecond counts. In the industrial field all controls, devices and machines on the factory floor require a secured real-time communication. This differs from the office area, where the consequence of a communication delay or communication failure between an office PC and a printer is annoying, but not really dangerous. The same kind of communication failure happening between a factory control system and a robot or a safety device on the factory floor may be really dangerous. It is obvious that for industrial use, secured and very fast communication is mandatory.

Digitalization in the industrial area can be successful only if open standards for secured and fast communication between devices, controls and all related computer systems is established. Therefore, an Industrial Internet has to offer standardized communication protocols for secured and fast communication. Further, in an Industrial Internet of Things, it should be possible by use of standard communication protocols to connect any devices from any vendors safely to each other without problems or additional effort.

4.4.2 *Time-Sensitive Networking (TSN)*

The Industrial Internet is moving towards the ethernet-based standard Time-Sensitive Networking (TSN), which provides significant advantages for automation applications in industries. The Institute of

Electrical and Electronics Engineers (IEEE) has extended the Ethernet standard within the framework of IEEE 802.1 by adding mechanisms for real-time communication. These include time-controlled transmission, synchronization and bandwidth reservation. This will enable the Ethernet to supply the same time information to all of the connected devices that support these extended standards. As a result, the entire network will be precisely synchronized. In addition, reservation protocols ensure that the data packets are transmitted from the sender to the destination via all the intervening switches according to a predefined timetable. As a result of the encapsulation of streams, TSN makes it possible to run multiple real-time protocols simultaneously in a single network.

With TSN it will be possible to transmit all data including real-time information through a single network simultaneously. TSN permits robust, reliable and standardized Ethernet communication between automation devices, even under extreme network loads. In future, fieldbus network infrastructures will be gradually upgraded to integrate basic TSN technology (Buck 2018).

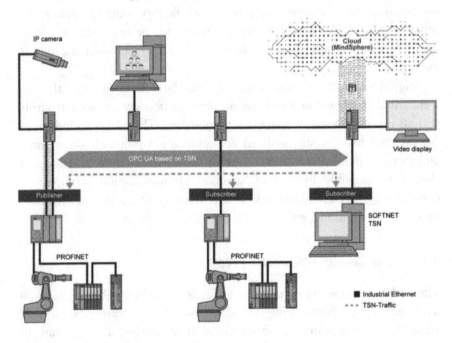

Fig. 4.4. TSN based Communication (Siemens 2018j, p. 2).

In addition to real-time communication within machines, with the use of TSN, the communication between machines can be performed in real time (Fig. 4.4). An Ethernet with TSN will be introduced into the digital enterprise processes and a single network will be enabled for all data. Using this technology, it will be possible to use standard hardware components for fieldbus real-time industrial communication protocols that are based on TSN. This will enable all data, including real-time information, to be transmitted through a single network in effect simultaneously (Siemens 2018j, p. 2).

4.4.3 *Open Platform Communications (OPC) Standard*

The Open Platform Communications (OPC) is an important standard on the way to digitalization. It specifies the parameters for the communication of real-time plant data between control devices from different manufacturers. OPC UA is platform neutral and provides proven security mechanisms and powerful performance. It enables seamless communication with applications from different parties and can flexibly be scaled to the required need. With its semantic capabilities, it supports intelligent and autonomous systems. With OPC UA it is possible to build open interfaces from the controller level up to the cloud.

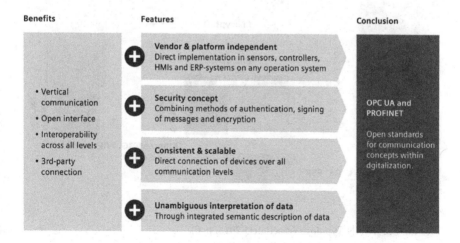

Fig. 4.5. Benefits and Features of OPC UA and PROFINET (Siemens 2017e).

Nowadays OPC UA can be combined with the advantages of Time-Sensitive Networking (TSN). This also combines the existing standards and optimizes Ethernet with an extended Quality of Service (QoS) mechanism, time synchronization, low transmission latencies and seamless redundancy.

4.4.4 *Long Range (LoRa) Technology*

Low Power Wide Area Networks (LPWAN) offer us the possibility of connecting wireless edge devices at low power and low cost. LoRaWAN defines the communication protocol and system architecture for the network while the LoRa physical layer enables the long-range communication link from the bottom up to optimize LPWANs for battery lifetime, capacity, range and cost. LoRa Technology offers a mix of long range, low power consumption and secure data transmission. Public and private networks using this technology can provide coverage that is greater in range compared to that of existing cellular networks. This technology is easy to plug into the existing infrastructure and offers a solution to serve battery-operated IIoT applications.

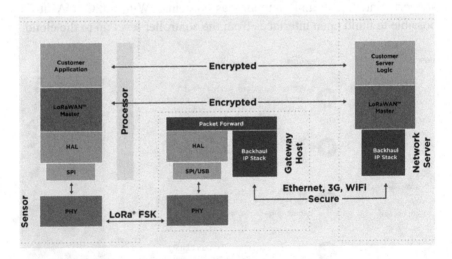

Fig. 4.6. LoRaWAN Typology (machineQ 2018, p. 6).

This wireless communication takes advantage of the long-range characteristics of the LoRa physical layer, allowing a single-hop link between the end-device and one or many gateways. It uses unlicensed radio spectrum in the Industrial, Scientific and Medical (ISM) bands to enable low power, wide area communication between remote sensors and the connection of gateways to the network. The protocol is designed specifically for low power consumption, extending battery lifetime, range and security through embedded end-to-end encryption. All modes are capable of bi-directional communication and there is support for multicast addressing groups to make efficient use of the spectrum during tasks. Through the LoRaWAN the end nodes and gateways can be connected and the information transmitted into the cloud for use in related applications (LoRa Alliance 2015).

4.4.5 *Device-to-Cloud-and-back Connectivity*

A device-to-cloud solution provides an enterprise IIoT platform that enables device lifecycle management, analytics and application integration to drive digital transformation. Sensors, devices and systems form the connection between the physical and digital worlds.

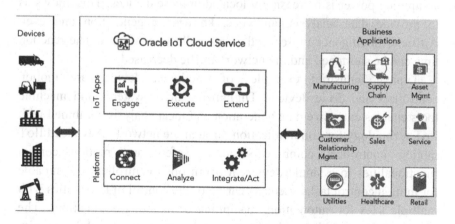

Fig. 4.7. IoT Cloud Service Functional Representation (SystemsOracle 2016, p. 5).

Connecting the edge to the enterprise with a properly designed end-to-end IIoT solution can efficiently provide data and device visibility in order to increase operational efficiency. IIoT cloud services have to bridge the gap between edge devices and applications and to securely connect all IIoT devices, collect data, analyze these data and integrate them with enterprise applications and processes. When the right data is available for the right application at the right time using open interfaces and pre-integrations, they can be the basis for real-time big data and predictive analytics to be performed. These processes deliver enriched data that enables us to identify new services and system improvements. Data-enriched enterprise applications and processes are required and can be offered as software-as-a-service (SaaS) or platform-as-a-service (PaaS) (Oracle 2016b, p. 1).

4.4.6 *Intelligent Devices*

Intelligent devices which deliver and receive data from the network are the basis of any IIoT application. These devices can be classified into sensors delivering data and actors receiving data. Most industrial assets include sensors and actors. As edge computing becomes more popular, computing power is increasingly located in these devices. This allows us to provide data analysis, analytics, knowledge generation and even Artificial Intelligence closer to the data collection sources. The reaction time can be shortened and the network traffic decreased.

Typical industrial examples of intelligent devices are motion controllers and drive devices. Digitalizing drive systems and machine tools enables extensive data generation and local analysis combined with IIoT technology for communication through the network. Advanced IIoT motion controllers combine standard, safety and motion control functionalities in a single device. Modern open controllers are suitable for motion control tasks such as gearing or the control of kinematics with multiple axes for automation, machining or handling applications. The motion of selected kinematics in space can be monitored with kinematics libraries using fail-safe technology in combination with automation controls in order to protect the machine operator during work. The speed of selected points, such as the tool center point, and freely configurable zones, such as the working and protection areas, can be monitored through the IIoT.

Fig. 4.8. Advanced IIoT Motion Controller (Siemens 2018g).

In modern servo drive systems, servomotors can be connected to converters using a one cable connection for power and communication. Through the use of IIoT technology and extended safety functions the converter can be activated via a web server. The interaction between servomotors, quick sampling and smart control algorithms using high quality encoder systems and low rotor inertia to provide drive systems with highly dynamic and accurate data allows dynamic control, making sure that loads can be moved dynamically. Further safety functions have to ensure that machine functions have been provided with comprehensive protection (Siemens 2017b).

4.4.7 *IIoT-Applications using Cloud-Based Services*

With open IIoT technology, apps for the asset monitoring and control of devices in IIoT systems can offer user interfaces with advanced features for the control and operation of nearly any device in a digital enterprise environment. These apps use cloud-based services which provide enterprises with open IIoT operation systems to connect with the particular devices.

Relevant data can be accessed from production devices for analysis in the cloud. Messages about the actual performance and device status are received from the cloud and feedback controls are also sent to the devices. In order to simplify the design and deployment of IIoT applications, there are mainly three components to be considered. The applications have to include an interface to monitor events or the statuses or locations of assets and to interact with the devices for control purposes. This interfacing is performed through the IIoT operating systems. The core of the application includes the data model and business logic, and depending on the application, contextual data, predictive algorithms or machine learning algorithms. The application can be customized and configured for specific business needs using application frameworks (SystemsOracle 2016).

IIoT apps are applicable for a wide range of use cases. The market for IIoT apps is still young and in future the range of available applications will expand widely. Examples of apps for machine monitoring, analysis and remote control and the analysis of drives will be shown. Modern machine monitoring apps connect with machines and systems to analyze and visualize relevant data.

Fig. 4.9. Machine Monitoring App (Siemens 2017f).

The apps create transparency regarding the status and performance of the machines and enable services to be optimized. The operational and maintenance status of machine devices is monitored in terms of productivity, servicing and availability. User-definable views allow us to customize and filter data according to specific criteria and to access alarms and messages individually. These alarms and messages can be accessed by particular users or user groups from any location.

The focus of the monitoring apps is on improving the availability and productivity of manufacturing facilities through higher transparency by calculating, analyzing and visualizing actual and historical data. The apps can provide users with guidance for decision-making in order to improve efficiency and to optimize systems.

Fig. 4.10. Analysis and Remote Control of Machines (Siemens 2018k, p. 4).

The remote control of the Computerized Numerical Control (CNC) machines by use of IIoT apps enables remote access to these machines by means of failsafe encrypted communication through the Internet. This access improves machine availability and simplifies maintenance as it allows us to record the required maintenance process. These apps connect to the IIoT operating system, providing machine operators with a cloud-based overview of the operating status across all connected CNC machines. Such apps allow relevant machine data to be captured, analyzed and visualized in order to improve user transparency with regard to the current CNC machine status and its development (Siemens 2018k, p. 2).

IIoT apps for drives and machine tools provide applications which enable innovative digital services such as predictive maintenance, energy data management or resource optimization. These apps are connected to an open IIoT operating system which allows users to utilize the benefits of cloud-based services and create added value with machine operation, improving the efficiency and productivity of drive systems and machines across the production network.

Fig. 4.11. Analysis of Drives App (Siemens 2018k, p. 3).

By using apps to analyze drives, the machine operators are able to monitor drive components of machines. These apps capture and analyze operating data, and detect actual maintenance requirements by continuously monitoring power consumption, torque and frequency. The machine operators are kept informed about critical situations and machine builders are able to offer preventive servicing on demand, which reduces the probability of unscheduled costs and minimizes downtimes in order to improve machine capacity utilization and productivity.

The energy management of production systems is increasingly an important issue and the measurement of energy flows can determine energy-saving potential (Siemens 2018k, p. 1). As part of monitoring in digital enterprises, energy-managing apps have to provide mobile recordings of consumption data and energy transparency. With increasing requirements regarding material-related energy analyses, baseline management or energy consumption forecasts, an energy-managing app has to offer comprehensive analytical possibilities. Additional interfaces, such as an energy efficiency monitor for assessing the efficiency of machines and plants, are typical features of these apps (Siemens 2017f).

4.5 Data Analytics and Integration

Data are the heart of the disruptions occurring across economies and enterprises and can be recognized as an increasingly critical corporate asset. The volume of available data has grown exponentially, due to the fact that methods for generating, collecting and storing data have fundamentally changed. Data proliferation from various sources creating torrents of information. In fact, because so much of the world is instrumented, it is actually difficult to avoid generating data (Henke *et al.* 2016, p. 22). Nowadays, the critical point is how to use the data (Fig. 4.12) to create value from raw data up to prescriptive techniques.

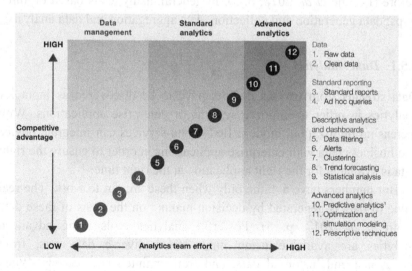

Fig. 4.12. Analytics Strategies Generating Value (Levene *et al.* 2018, p. 3).

Data and analytics are used in all industries, but an even bigger wave will come when deep learning reaches maturity, giving machines unprecedented capabilities (Henke *et al.* 2016, p. 79).

Data have to be managed across all platforms including the cloud. This can be done by adapting an appropriate data management infrastructure to hybrid multiplatform data architectures. It is important to get organized and to deploy substantial data management infrastructure before migrating data and its management to the cloud.

Analytics techniques are increasingly being used to discover patterns in huge amounts of data, and to generate new hypotheses through finding new patterns. The application of data and analytics, including supervised and unsupervised machine learning, Artificial Intelligence and deep learning, to product, design and process innovation is still in the early stages and will increase significantly in future.

Advanced analytics can take advantage of data-driven environments and has the ability to generate valuable insights from large amounts of data. Analytics has emerged as a powerful approach that allows us to learn from past performance in order to more accurately predict trends. It creates value when big data and advanced algorithms are applied to business problems to yield a solution that is measurably better than before (Levene *et al.* 2018, p. 3). In general, analytics is based on three steps: data generation and collection, data aggregation and data analysis.

4.5.1 *Data Analytics*

Data streams from various devices have to be discovered as input for analytics in order to improve systems or enterprise applications. With increasing digitization, modern IIoT-cloud-services can integrate device and business data with enterprise applications in order to ensure the right data is available for the right application at the right time.

But numbers have a value only when these are put to work. The real value of data is generated by decision-making on the basis of these data (Chin *et al.* 2017, p. 5). Powerful analytics tools using advanced analytics are available using inputs from diverse data sets, from operational and historical data, and from maintenance records. When these are combined with processing systems and machine learning, predictive insights can be created.

An effective transformation strategy can be broken down into several components (Fig. 4.13). The first step should be to ask some fundamental questions to shape the strategic vision: What shall data and analytics be used for? How shall the insights drive value? How shall the value be measured? The second element is to build out the underlying data architecture as well as data collection or generation capabilities. Digital enterprises require us to switch from classical data systems to more flexible architectures when storing and analyzing big data. These may also need to digitize operations completely, in order to capture more data from equipment, internal processes and customer interactions or supply networks.

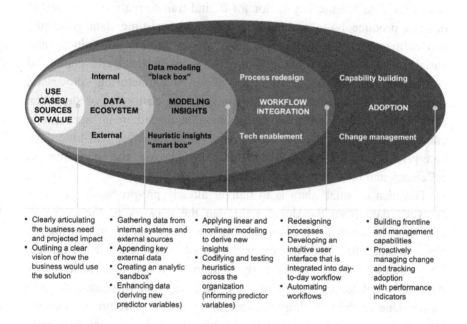

Fig. 4.13. Elements of Data and Analytics Transformation (Henke *et al.* 2016, p. 4).

We need to acquire analytical capabilities in order to derive insights from data. Enterprises may choose to add in-house capabilities or outsource to specialists. Changing business processes to incorporate data insights into the actual workflow requires getting the right data insights into the hands of the right people. Finally, enterprises need to build the capabilities of executives and mid-level managers so that they understand how to use data-driven insights and to rely on these for decision-making (Henke *et al.* 2016, p. 3).

The integration between cloud-based analytics and cloud- and premise-based business applications enable insights from of real-time IIoT data to be put fast to work. This integration enables advanced process optimization involving multiple processes, systems and predictive analytics (Turner 2016).

4.5.2 *Smart Data / Big Data*

Real-time data are the key factor for digital transformations. Connected devices produce huge amounts of data, and real-time data generated across manufacturing networks have grown rapidly in volume and variety. These data are coming directly from products and connected production or logistic equipment, core manufacturing processes, enterprise IT systems and external sources from customers or suppliers. Data in themselves have no real value, but placed in an appropriate context, data can be used to create new value. By using real-time data, enterprises can create new insights and increase the performance, efficiency and reliability of the processes and facilities.

The idea of smart data is to deliver already pre-processed and pre-analyzed data from the devices through the network to the decision-making unit. Smart devices are equipped with sensors for measuring the physical state, the performance or the possible problems of the device. The resulting values are properly analyzed by use of algorithms or Artificial Intelligence locally in the device, in order to reduce network traffic. Due to the very high number of sensors in enterprises systems, the smart data concept has a lot of advantages for digital enterprise concepts. Data from smart, connected products can generate insights that help us to optimize product, production or logistic performance. The smart data concept enables us to improve automation through the use of self-diagnostic, self-learning and condition-based maintenance systems.

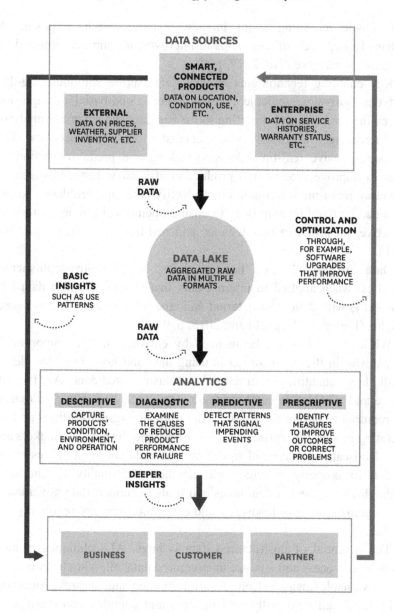

Fig. 4.14. Creating New Value with Data (Porter and Heppelmann 2015, p. 9).

Big Data Analytics is a relatively new technique for managing and analyzing very large data sets by use of statistical models for probabilistic reasoning about images, text or speech. Exposing AI systems to large sets of data helps to improve and train decision-making processes (Gramatke *et al.* 2017, p. 9).

Key enabling technologies include data-capture solutions, big-data analytics software, scalable, cost-efficient cloud-based storage and processing facilities and reporting tools. Big data and advanced analytics are increasingly accessible via specialist cloud-based services. This drives responsive real-time decision-making and predictive actions in order to improve product and production efficiency. Embedded sensors will relay real-time information and identify emerging problems, so that these can be fixed preemptively to ensure operational efficiency through proactive, preventative maintenance and real-time reaction (Atos 2016, p. 11).

Data analytics reveals basic insights, while more sophisticated analytics, when applied to internal data that is pooled into a data lake (Fig. 4.14) with data from external and enterprise sources, offers deeper insights (Porter and Heppelmann 2015, p. 9).

While data lakes are being used by enterprises, it is important to clarify who in the organization is using data and how. How should we handle large quantities of structured and unstructured data? Are the data secure and reliable? Several strategic steps, including data governance, are required to define the strategy, the roles, the responsibilities and the operating model. Enterprises have to define who the decision makers are. Data landscapes are needed to define standards and data processes are needed to properly manage and maintain the quality of the data. Technologies to design data lakes and tools to support data governance, data organization, data landscape and data processing are required (Atos 2018a).

The potential of unstructured data is huge. AI techniques make it possible to process and analyze unstructured data, allowing businesses to obtain valuable insights from this information and improve decision-making. AI can potentially find patterns and complex relationships by shifting through billions of observations (Tressel *et al.* 2017). Data lake engines are key components to becoming data-driven. The rapid evolution of data systems leads us towards data-guided decision-making, transforming how companies organize, operate and manage their business to create value. In short, big data could generate big disruptions (Henke *et al.* 2016, p. 52).

4.5.3 *Data Quality and Reliability*

Data of high quality and reliability are the precondition for any improvement and also the key for the success of any AI use case. In order to be usable for decision-making, data must be delivered in a user-friendly manner to be analyzed and processed into information. Consequently, the first principle of information systems is that data should be prepared and processed in a manner that supports decision-making (Schuh *et al.* 2017, p. 24).

An important issue concerning data from various physical sensors and systems is the quality and reliability of these data. It is crucial to determine the type, quantity and quality of data. Therefore, in industrial application the systems have to apply anomaly detection to sensor data, using a combination of physics-based knowledge and collected sensor data. There are five types of technologies for anomaly detection available, and these are domain or physics-based methods, statistical process control, advanced signal processing, machine learning anomaly detectors and deep learning anomaly detection (General Electric Company 2016, p. 16). Domain or physics-based methods enable anomaly detection through the comparison of calculated parameters with measured values. Statistical process control, which uses univariate and multivariate control chart techniques, can also be used for detection. Advanced signal processing is a method to detect anomalies in the presence of sensor noise. Algorithms using wavelets, kernel regression and multi-sensor data fusion techniques may be applied. Machine learning anomaly detectors can be used, ranging from multivariate multi-level survival models to baseline asset risk to classification techniques like logistic regression, decision trees, random forest methods, neural networks and clustering methodologies. Deep learning neural networks can be trained to detect anomalies. This technology requires a long training phase. However, when the network is trained it can be applied to very complex problems and the training can be continued and the network enhanced before performing new detections.

4.6 Artificial Intelligence (AI)

Artificial Intelligence (AI) is concerned with getting computers to perform tasks that would normally require human intelligence. AI is the driving key technology creating waves of changes that will affect business, organizational and operational processes significantly in all areas of life. Artificial Intelligence can be defined as the ability of a machine to perform cognitive functions associated with human abilities, such as perceiving, reasoning, learning and problem solving.

Artificial Intelligence (AI) technologies have been developed since the 1950s, but due to the required computing power, AI and cognitive technologies have just recently taken off in business and technical applications (Gramatke *et al.* 2017, p. 3).

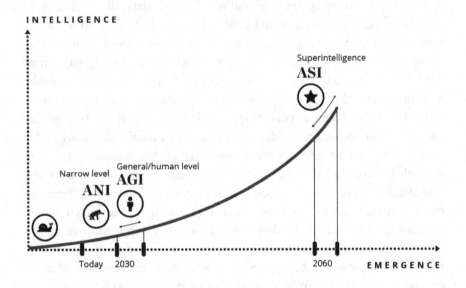

Fig. 4.15. How Smart is Artificial Intelligence (Deloitte 2017, p. 12)?

Current AI is still narrow. In a specific task Artificial Narrow Intelligence (ANI) can become as good as or even better than a human. However, each specific ANI application is still performing a very narrow, clearly defined task within its application area and is not able to build capabilities to learn tasks outside this application area. A chess computer could beat a human in playing chess, but that same computer failed at solving a complex mathematical problem. Google's ANI that beat the human champion of the Chinese board game Go would be unable to learn how to play chess without help, even though chess is significantly less complex than the game of Go (Deloitte 2017, p. 12).

Artificial Intelligence is moving from machine learning towards more advanced cognitive technologies. Cognitive technology augments human decision-making capabilities, while gradually performing certain judgment-based tasks independently in a manner similar to humans. Cognition is the ability to identify objects and structures and to understand and transcribe texts and speech. Cognitive software is based on the abilities of memory, learning and reasoning. Memory is required to hold and store knowledge. Learning is the ability to create knowledge about the environment that can be used for reasoning and reasoning is the ability to use knowledge about the environment in order to deduce conclusions from available information (Gramatke *et al.* 2017, p. 4).

Stage	Description

Robotics **Mimics Human** **Actions**	• Used for rule-based processes, such as invoice processing exceptions
	 • Addresses priority business problems driven by process breakages
	 • Enables
	   – Faster handling time
	   – Reduced handling costs
	   – Reduced error rates

Intelligent Automation **Mimics/Augments** **Quantitative Human Judgment**	• Processes requiring judgment such as commercial contract understanding, insights, and implications • Covers machine learning capability • Interprets human behavior
Cognitive Automation **Augments Human Intelligence**	• Used for predictive decision making, such as Amazon Echo and Alexa • Dynamically self-managing and adaptable
Artificial General Intelligence **Mimics Human Intelligence**	• Systems that completely replicate human capabilites • Turing Test Definition: "A test for intelligence in a computer, requiring that a human being should be unable to distinguish the machine from another human being by using the replies to questions put to both"

Fig. 4.16. Stages of AI (Gramatke *et al.* 2017, p. 5).

Nowadays AI has moved beyond the purely scientific and become central to digital transformation. AI enables organizations to synthesize vast amounts of structured and unstructured data, to query results in natural language and to apply machine-learning capabilities to data analysis. These capabilities can significantly enhance insights, efficiency and speed (Favilla *et al.* 2018, p. 3).

In digital enterprises, the use of Artificial Intelligence technologies will increase rapidly (Fig. 4.17). AI technology holds the potential to fundamentally redefine the industry on all levels, challenging business models. The advances of production technologies and factory processes enable new relationships with end-customers. Investment in AI is still in the early stages and a McKinsey study (Bughin *et al.* 2017, p. 12) estimates a large amount of use cases in machine learning, in computer vision and natural language, in autonomous vehicles, in smart robotics and in virtual agents.

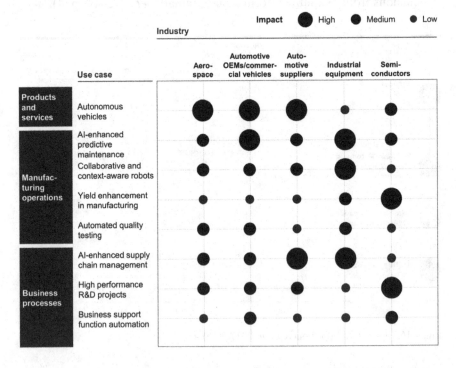

Fig. 4.17. Impact of AI Use Cases Across Multiple Industries (McKinsey 2017a, p. 19).

A study from IBM on the most-cited priorities for AI/cognitive investment in the next three years shows that the main issue is quality control. Other issues are analyzing data to avoid problems (66%), production planning, recommending performance improving actions (62%) and machine maintenance, identifying anomalies and assisting in repairs (50%) (Favilla *et al*. 2018, p. 4).

4.6.1 *Machine Learning*

Machine Learning (ML) is an application of Artificial Intelligence in which computers perform tasks by learning from data instead of by being explicitly programmed. The more data an algorithm can access, the more the algorithm can learn. Real-world machine learning examples are everywhere, such as personalized product recommendations from websites, facial recognition or fastest route suggestions in routing applications. Machine learning is still in the early stages of industrial development and implementation, but machine learning has enormous potential. It can be used to discover new signals in data that could allow for the continuous improvement of enterprise systems (SAP 2018a).

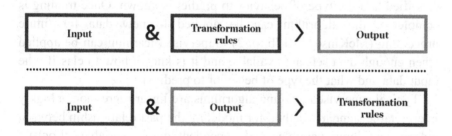

Fig. 4.18. Traditional Programming / Machine Learning (Deloitte 2017, p. 12).

In traditional programming and data science, transformation rules are defined to create output data based on input data. In contrast to the traditional approach, machine learning algorithms use training data and feedback to learn the transformation rules (Fig. 4.18). The principal steps for all types of machine learning are to acquire, to store and to analyze data and feed these data into a rule engine in order to train the learning algorithm. Machine learning can be applied to many different problems and data sets. It can be trained to identify pictures and potential fraud cases in insurance claims, or to transform handwriting into structured text or speech into text. All these examples require tagged training sets. Depending on the technique used, an algorithm can improve itself by adding a feedback loop.

Machine learning is based on data, either structured, or, increasingly, unstructured. The machine is not explicitly being programmed. Machine learning algorithms can be supervised learning, where the algorithm is trained using examples with input data and the correct answers. In unsupervised learning the algorithm must discover patterns in the data on its own. In reinforced learning the algorithm is rewarded or penalized for the actions it takes based on trial and error (McDermott 2018).

4.6.1.1 *Supervised Learning*

Supervised learning is the most common method for training ML algorithms today. Supervised learning algorithms use training data and feedback from humans to learn the relationship of outputs to given inputs. Supervised Learning is applicable when the input data can be classified and the type of behavior to predict is known. Once training is completed, the algorithm can be applied to new data for future processing (McKinsey 2017b, p. 2). Supervised learning can be applied when enough data sets are available and it is known how to classify the input data and what the type of behavior to predict is.

Typical supervised learning algorithms are linear regression, a highly interpretable standard method for modeling the past relationship between independent input variables and dependent output variables. Logistic regression is an extension of linear regression used for classification tasks. Linear/quadratic discriminant analysis upgrades a logistic regression to deal with nonlinear problems. Decision trees are highly interpretable classification or regression models that split data-feature values into branches at decision nodes. Naive Bayes is a classification technique that applies Bayes theorem. Support vector machine is a technique typically used for classification transformed to perform regression. Random forest is a classification or regression model that improves the accuracy of a simple decision tree by generating multiple decision trees. AdaBoost uses a multitude of models as a classification or regression technique. Gradient-boosting trees are a classification or regression technique that generates decision trees sequentially and simple neural networks models in which artificial neurons move through an input layer, a hidden layer, where calculations take place, and an output layer (McKinsey 2017, pp. 3-4).

4.6.1.2 *Unsupervised Learning*

With unsupervised learning the machine learning algorithm explores input data without being given explicit output variables. The algorithm identifies concepts and derives conclusions entirely on its own Unsupervised Learning can be applied to unstructured data and the algorithm will find patterns and classify the data. The algorithm receives unlabeled data, creates a structure from the data and identifies groups of data that exhibit similar behavior. Unsupervised learning can be used when it is not known how to classify the data.

Typical unsupervised learning algorithms are K-means clustering, which involves putting data into a number of groups determined by the model such that each contains data with similar characteristics. The Gaussian mixture model is a generalization of K-means clustering that provides more flexibility in the size and shape of groups. Hierarchical clustering splits or aggregates clusters along a hierarchical tree to form a classification system and the Recommender system uses cluster behavior prediction to identify the important data necessary for making a recommendation (McKinsey 2017b, p. 5).

4.6.1.3 *Reinforcement Learning*

Reinforcement learning is typically applied if there are not much training data. The way to learn about the environment is to interact with it. The algorithm takes action in the environment and receives feedback that ascertains if the action brings the system a step closer to the goal. It optimizes for the best series of actions by correcting itself over time. Over time, the algorithm learns to produce the correct output, based on learning from the reinforcement of correct answers and facing punishment for incorrect ones. As long as the learning environment is representative of the physical-world problem the performance of the algorithm improves with repetition, in many cases even surpassing human capabilities. Reinforcement learning takes actions towards a specified goal, but without direction on which actions to take in order to get there. The algorithms explore a broad range of possible actions while gradually learning which ones are most effective, thereby incorporating an element of creativity.

Reinforcement learning has been applied to applications ranging from learning how to play games like chess and Go to improving logistics management (Henke *et al.* 2016, p. 24). Reinforcement learning has been very successful in training computers to play games in conjunction with deep-learning techniques. In 2017 it enabled the AI system AlphaGo to defeat world champion Ke Jie in the game of Go. The system AlphaGo Zero, which was using a new form of reinforcement learning, defeated its predecessor AlphaGo after learning to play Go from scratch, starting with completely random play against itself rather than training on Go games played by and with humans (Chui, Manyika, and Miremadi 2018, p. 4).

4.6.1.4 *Machine Learning Requirements*

Not every application can benefit from machine learning. There is very much potential in applications that have complex rules and large amounts of data. There are some basic requirements for machine learning. Machine learning needs a specific, well defined task, where the relevant inputs and desired output can be clearly stated. Depending on the machine learning type, a sufficient quantity of examples to learn from and significant meaningful differences within the dataset may be required in order to provide useful results. Current machine learning requires training data sets that are not only labeled but also sufficiently large and comprehensive with thousands of data points. To become relatively good at classification tasks and to perform at the level of humans, millions of records are required (Chui, Manyika, and Miremadi 2018, p. 5). Then machine learning can be valuable in discovering correlations in large amounts of data that humans could never have deduced for themselves.

However, it is mandatory to focus on specific tasks. It is not possible to learn from all the data in the enterprise automatically. Unsupervised or semi-supervised approaches reduce the need for large, labeled data sets. Two promising techniques are reinforcement learning and generative adversarial networks.

4.6.2 *Neuronal Networks / Deep Learning*

Neuronal networks are computer models for deep learning which are built in analogy to the human brain. Neural networks are a subset of machine learning techniques based on how neurons interact in the human brain. The machine learning algorithms use multiple layers of nodes operating in parallel to learn, recognize patterns and make decisions. AI practitioners refer to these techniques as deep learning, since neural networks have many layers of simulated interconnected neurons. Before deep learning, simple neural networks often had only three to five layers and some neurons. Deep learning uses neural networks that include many layers of neurons and a huge volume of data, with simulated neurons numbering into the millions (Chui, Manyika, Miremadi, Henke, Chung, Nel, Pieter, and Malhotra 2018a, p. 4).

Deep learning is a type of machine learning that can process a wide range of data resources, requires less data preprocessing by humans and can often produce more accurate results than traditional machine-learning approaches. This advanced type of machine learning can solve complex, non-linear problems and is responsible for AI breakthroughs such as natural language processing, personal digital assistants and self-driving cars.

Neuronal networks can be classified into Feed Forward Neural Networks (FFNNs), Convolutional Neural Networks (CNNs), Recurrent Neural Networks (RNNs) and Generative Adversarial Networks (GANs). All of these networks learn through the use of training data and backpropagation algorithms (Chui, Manyika, Miremadi, Henke, Chung, Nel, Pieter, and Malhotra 2018b, p. 3).

4.6.2.1 *Feed Forward Neural Networks*

Feed Forward Neural Networks (FFNNs) had already been proposed in 1958 and are still one of the most common types of artificial neural network. In these networks the information always moves in the forward direction, from the input layer, through the hidden layers, to the output layer. There are no loops in the network.

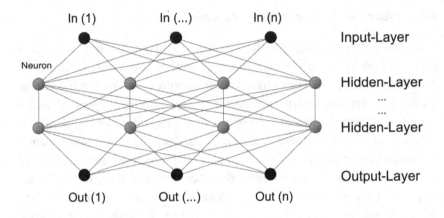

Fig. 4.19. Neuronal Network.

The neurons are moving in a deep learning neural network (Fig. 4.19) from an input-layer through some hidden layer towards an output layer. The input data are processed through multiple interconnected hidden layers, and increasingly complex features of the data are learned at each layer. Based on this learning the network makes a determination about the data, learns if the determination is correct and then uses what has been learned to make determinations about new data. For example, once a network has learned what an object looks like, it can recognize the object in new images (McKinsey 2017b, p. 6).

4.6.2.2 *Convolutional Neural Networks*

Convolutional Neural Networks (CNNs) are artificial neural networks suited for visual perception tasks in which the connections between neural layers are inspired by the organization of the visual cortex, the portion of the brain that processes images. These multilayered neural networks are designed to extract increasingly complex features of the data at each layer to determine the output and can be used to gather information from unstructured data sets. The network consists of an input, an output and multiple hidden layers. The hidden layers of a CNN typically consist of convolutional layers, pooling layers, fully connected layers and normalization layers. After learning, the neural network can classify the unique features previously identified from input data sets.

Convolutional neural networks are mostly applied to the analysis of visual images. Individual neurons respond to stimuli only in a restricted region of the visual field. CNNs learn to filter information and use relatively little pre-processing compared to image classification algorithms. The independence from prior knowledge and human effort is a major advantage. Typical applications are image and video recognition, recommender systems, image classification, technical and medical image analysis and natural language processing (McKinsey 2017b, p. 7).

4.6.2.3 *Recurrent Neural Networks*

Recurrent Neural Networks (RNNs) are artificial neural networks whose connections between neurons include loops, which are well-suited for processing sequences of inputs. This makes the algorithms highly effective in a wide range of applications, from handwriting to text or speech recognition. These multilayered neural networks can store information in context nodes, allowing them to learn data sequences and to output a number or another sequence. These networks can be used when working with time-series data or sequences. The neuron receives an information that indicates the start of a sequence, then the next element of a sequence and outputs a vector of numbers that feeds back into the neuron to remember the information received. The same process occurs when it receives any next element of a sequence with the state of the neuron updating upon receiving each element. After receiving the last element, the neuron assigns a probability to every element from a possible vocabulary that could complete the sequence. If trained well, the neural network will choose the element with the highest probability to continue the sequence (McKinsey 2017b, p. 7).

4.6.2.4 *Generative Adversarial Networks (GANs)*

Generative Adversarial Networks (GANs) use two neural networks contesting each other in a zero-sum game framework. GANs can learn to mimic various distributions of data, such as text, speech and images. The networks are therefore valuable in generating test datasets when these are not readily available. In this semi-supervised learning method, two networks compete against each other to improve and refine understanding of a concept. The ability of GANs to generate increasingly believable examples of data can significantly reduce the need for data sets labeled by humans. Training an algorithm to identify different types of images would typically require millions of human-labeled images with the type or at the stage of a given image. By using GANs, researchers could train a specific detection algorithm that combines a much smaller human-labeled data set with the GAN's output.

While the application of GANs in precise diagnoses is still a way off, researchers have started using GANs in increasingly sophisticated contexts including satellite imagery, along with an understanding of geographical features, to create up-to-date maps of rapidly developing areas (Chui, Manyika, and Miremadi 2018, p. 5).

4.6.3 *Evolutionary Optimization*

Evolutionary optimization is a population-based stochastic search technique. In this field the most common techniques are genetic algorithms which offer a promising optimization approach for the improvement of technical solutions in complex enterprises. These algorithms follow the approach of evolution in nature, as they are very flexible and can adapt to nearly any environment. The biological evolution has the ability to adapt complex structures and organisms to different environmental conditions by the mechanism of variation of the genetic material and an applied selection mechanism. The population with the best adaption (phenotype) to the environment will survive through generations. Learning from nature, we can apply similar mathematical genetic algorithms to improve technical systems.

Mathematical genetic algorithms are a formal abstraction of the mutation and selection mechanism discovered by Darwin. The variable vector represents the inheritance information (genotype) of an individual and the system parameter represents the elements of their DNA. In analogy to the biology, it is assumed that a parent vector will generate new child vectors through random variation. For each generation by use of the model a fitness value is calculated, which represents the phenotypes, or the vitality, of the particular individual. The fitness function represents the selection mechanism which decides if an individual will survive or not. Through this selection, it is decided which vector will be a parent of the next generation. Multi-dimensional evolutionary strategies offer a high potential for parallelization and are reliable optimization methods with good convergence behavior for complex problems, especially if advanced inheritance mechanisms, such as crossing over, are implemented. Similarly to the adaption of biological systems to a specific environment, mathematical evolutionary strategies can adapt to specific environments. Besides the algorithm of the fitness function there is no other specific information about the environment required.

4.6.4 *Cognitive Computing*

Cognitive computing refers to next-generation information systems that use artificially intelligent technologies, analytics and data to understand, reason, learn and interact. A cognitive system is capable of extracting information from unstructured data by extracting concepts and relationships into a knowledge base. This is possible as cognitive systems can use contextual information, understand unstructured data and reason about information. These systems can communicate with humans through many media, including speech, image, video, sign language, graphs or any combination of these.

Cognitive systems can build knowledge and learn, understand natural language, reason and interact more naturally with human beings than traditional programmable systems. AI solutions have some, but not necessarily all, of the intelligent characteristics of cognitive systems. Automation has advanced from merely moving data to commanding complex systems, which includes performing judgment-based, AI-enabled interactions (IBM 2017b, p. 2).

4.6.5 *Opportunities and Limitations of AI*

The limitations in using deep learning algorithms are in the fields of data labeling, obtaining massive training data sets, explaining decisions and generalizing learning. Most machine learning algorithms require large amounts of training data in order to learn. The algorithms recognize patterns in the training data to develop an internal model of the system being described by the data. Reinforcement learning is slightly different than the other techniques as the training data are not given to the algorithm, but rather generated in real time via interactions with feedback from the environment (Henke *et al.* 2016, p. 82).

Most current algorithms are trained through supervised learning and humans have to label and categorize the underlying data. Unsupervised or semi-supervised approaches reduce the need for large, labeled data sets. Deep-learning methods call for large amounts of data records so that models can become relatively good at classification. Potential problems can arise when humans have to decide which data points to use and which to disregard. Some promising techniques are reinforcement learning and generative adversarial networks.

The ability to explain the reasons behind decisions is a general problem for most AI algorithms. Deep learning trains networks to make decisions, but it is not possible to retrace how a particular decision has been reached. This is one reason why the use of AI tools remain relatively low in areas where decisions have to be explainable for security or regulatory requirements.

A general learning approach, similar to human learning, is a problem for AI models. Most AI algorithms have difficulties transferring experiences from one set of use cases to another. In effect, whatever a model has achieved for a given use case remains applicable to that use case only. As a result, enterprises must repeatedly commit resources to train another model, even when the use cases are very similar. Possible approaches to this challenge are transfer learning, where an AI model is trained to accomplish a certain task and then applies that learning to a similar but distinct activity alternative, or the use of a generalized structure that can be applied to multiple problems (Chui, Manyika, and Miremadi 2018, pp. 3-9).

Machine learning forms the basis of most AI systems. But while a machine-learning system may look intelligent, as suggested by the definition of AI, in fact machine-learning algorithms are really not intelligent (Anon. 2017). A machine learning algorithm will never understand what it was trained to do. The algorithm is able to identify specific objects, but it will not know what the objects are or understand why these should be identified. And if there is a new sort of object emerging, it will probably not be able to identify it unless the algorithm is retrained.

Currently most AI algorithms are narrow AI performing a specific task, such as image recognition or optimizing logistic decisions. Even if machine learning for the specific use case beats human abilities, the algorithms fail on other tasks. Humans can specialize in many specific topics, from abstract mathematics to psychology to art, and can transfer knowledge from one area to another and become experts at all of these. The holy grail of AI is a general AI, a single system that can learn and then solve any problem with which it is presented (Anon. 2017). As machine learning and AI have huge potential and will expand influence in modern societies, the question of whether machines are capable of making ethical decisions arises.

4.7 Enterprise Security and Data Protection

Digital connectivity is making life easier and more comfortable and it also increases business competitiveness and creates significant economic potential. At the same time digitalization trends are producing new opportunities for attacks and vulnerabilities to occur. Digitalization and cybersecurity are two sides of the same coin and digitalization is the reason why cybersecurity has increasingly become a critical factor for business. Cyber criminals are increasingly attacking industrial facilities and attempting to find gaps in security walls. Damaging cyberattacks and streams of suspicious digital communications have made cybersecurity a top concern (Boehm *et al.* 2018, p. 2).

Enterprises face a challenging dilemma. Information has to be shared extensively as part of the collaborative processes, while at the same time the intellectual property rights and financial and business issues have to be protected. A prerequisite for the digital transformation is that cyber security and industrial security guarantee high security standards for data and connected systems (Aras 2016, p. 2).

The risk for enterprise security never ends. Therefore a cycle of identifying, analyzing and treating and monitoring risks has to be performed continuously and this never ends. A holistic approach to cybersecurity can address the lack of structure, lack of clarity, lack of consistent real-time data and the implications for governance, organizational structures and processes, controls, assets and people. The goal is to empower organizations to focus their defenses on the most likely and most threatening cyber risk scenarios, achieving a balance between effective security and efficient operations. Tight controls have to be applied to the most crucial assets (Boehm *et al.* 2018, p. 3).

Planning security
An ideal protection strategy for industrial systems is based on thorough planning.

Implementing security
Effective protection against cyber attacks is based on the rigorous implementation of technical and organizational measures.

Always active
Staying secure means staying active – continuously. Learn how Siemens protects its own products and solutions against cyber attacks.

Fig. 4.20. Holistic Protection of Industrial Plants (Siemens 2018j).

Security strategies have to be planned, implemented and kept always active. The holistic protection of industrial plants (Fig. 4.20) requires industrial security based on several lines of defense. A comprehensive security concept is required, which provides the enterprise with protection based on plant security, network security and system integrity according to the recommendations of the security standard IEC 62443 (Fig. 4.21) for industrial automation (Siemens 2018j, p. 2). Enterprise security has to put a combination of several obstacles in place against potential attackers to make attacks more difficult, time consuming and unsuccessful.

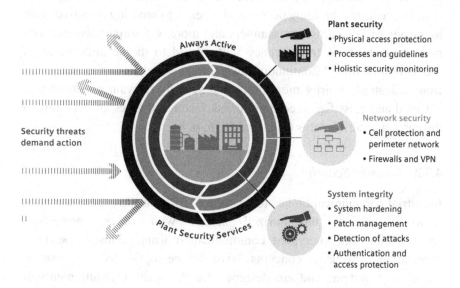

Fig. 4.21. Security Concept according to IEC 62443 (Siemens 2018j, p. 2).

To safeguard industrial facilities three basic steps are required. First, general plant security covers the physical access to the plant, which includes organizational measures such as security policies and monitoring the plant for anomalies that could indicate a cyberattack. The second is safeguarding networks including the installation of firewalls and the encryption of data transmission. The third focuses on system integrity, protecting the individual systems from access by unauthorized individuals as well as preventing unauthorized changes from being made (Siemens 2018j). A comprehensive concept according to IEC 62443 has to protect industrial plants from internal and external cyber attacks on all levels simultaneously.

4.7.1 *Plant Security*

Plant Security focuses on the physical protection and security management of the plant. Plant security has to prevent unauthorized persons from gaining physical access to critical components. This starts with conventional building access and extends to securing sensitive areas by means of key cards, iris scanners and more. Comprehensive security monitoring leads to transparency with regard to the security status of production facilities. Continuous analysis and correlation of existing data from industrial security monitoring and security-relevant events can be detected and classified according to risk factor and gives an overview of the current security status (Siemens 2016, p. 8).

4.7.2 *Network Security*

Industrial communication has to be secured by protecting the automation networks against unauthorized access with access protection, segmentation and encrypted communication using industrial security applications. Security concepts have to be optimized for use in automation systems and are designed for the specific requirements of industrial networks (Agarwal 2018, p. 12). Network security focuses on protecting networks from unauthorized access. This includes the monitoring of all interfaces and can be accomplished by means of firewalls and by establishing secured and protected demilitarized zones, which are used for making data available to other networks without granting direct access to the internal network itself. The security-related segmentation of the plant network into individually protected automation cells minimizes risks and increases security. Cell division and device assignment are based on communication and protection requirements. The communication nodes have to be securely authenticated and data transmission can be encrypted using a Virtual Private Network (VPN) to protect it from data espionage and manipulation.

To safeguard connected devices, some layers of security have to be considered and applied depending on the device and its associated risk. Device authentication has to ensure that the device hardware and software are authenticated when trying to access the network and verified before receiving or transmitting data. User access controls build mandatory or role-based access controls and password policies to limit user access to device components and applications. Application access controls limit which applications can access a device and securely monitor data sent to the device. Device lifecycle management has to implement procedures that enable devices to get timely security patches and updates to firmware and software. Data encryption has to protect configuration bit streams with encryption and to implement secure cryptographic key storage and zeroization capabilities (Cisco 2017, p. 5).

4.7.3 *System Integrity*

System integrity has to protect all devices against cyber-attacks and unauthorized access. The emphasis is on protecting automation systems and control components against unauthorized access. With a rise in IIoT attacks, enterprises must be more aware about confidential and sensitive data. In automated systems, single data points can trigger multiple actions and responses, and enterprises must be confident that the data have not been maliciously compromised, altered or falsified. Data encryption and decryption secure the digital value chain and provide additional protection. This requires the integration of industry-compatible security devices for system integrity in order to efficiently safeguard and protect industrial plants and automation systems. System integrity also involves authentication of users, access and change authorizations (Siemens 2016, p. 15).

4.7.4 *Blockchain Technology*

Blockchain is a technology that enables efficient, secure, immutable, trusted transactions among different parties, making it possible to eliminate intermediaries (Agarwal 2018, p. 3). Blockchain technology enables the creation of a decentralized environment, where the cryptographically validated transactions and data are not under the control of any third-party organization. Any transaction ever completed is recorded in an immutable ledger in a verifiable, secure, transparent and permanent way, with a timestamp and other details.

Blockchain is essentially a sequential, distributed ledger of transactions that is constantly updated and shared on a global network of computers. The ownership and history of a transaction is embedded in the blockchain at the transaction's earliest stages and verified at every subsequent stage. This makes it possible for every computer in the network to verify the transactions safely and transparently. Each computer node in the network holds a copy of the ledger, so there is no single point of failure. Every piece of information is mathematically encrypted and various consensus protocols are used to validate a new block before adding to the chain. This prevents fraud or double spending without requiring a central authority. The ledger can also be programmed with smart contracts, a set of conditions to trigger transactions automatically (Carson *et al.* 2018, p. 3).

The important element of block chain technology that maintains the strength of the blockchain is hashing. Each newly added block is encoded with a hash, an arithmetically produced code that is generated from the data contained within the block. Hashing is a well-known method used to secure passwords. The hash of the new block contains the hash of the previous block. This makes it extremely difficult to falsify new or existing parts of the blockchain since the hash of a previous block determines, in part, the hash of future blocks. In order to change one block, the entire blockchain would need to be rewritten (White 2017).

Through this the blockchain technology offers a shared, distributed and decentralized technology, which enables the safe exchange of data without a central verifying partner. This makes transactions faster and less expensive. The blockchain has the ability to change the way data are stored, shared and managed. The most powerful aspects of the technology are the barriers to changing or deleting information which has been added to the chain. It simplifies recordkeeping by establishing a single, authoritative view of the truth across all parties by building a secure, immutable history and chain of relevant information.

The blockchain technology can provide the foundation of automated trust for all parties in a supply network. Data about status, locations and transactions that has been generated from small devices and transferred to large machines can be recorded on the blockchain. Every manufactured object can be smart, connected and able to communicate so that it can be tracked and traced as needed. All information becomes irrefutably verifiable by all involved parties. In future production and logistic networks, blockchain technology will enable us to authenticate, track and trace, and automate transactions and interactions inside and between enterprises in order to secure flexible supply chains by ensuring the trustworthiness of data. Blockchain is adding trust, in an automated sense, and allows various parties to conduct commercial and technical transactions. It can act as a secured base for manufacturers to transmit encrypted information for additive manufacturing in tightly protected locations.

The core advantages of blockchains are decentralization, cryptographic security, transparency and immutability. They allow information to be verified and value to be exchanged without having to rely on a third-party authority. Self-sovereignty allows users to identify themselves and maintain control over the storage and management of data. Trust is offered through the technical infrastructure which ensures transparency to perform transactions in the knowledge that each party has the capacity to enter into that transaction. Immutability ensures that records are written and stored permanently, without the possibility of modification. There is no need for a central controlling authority to manage transactions or keep records and all parties can transact directly without the need for third-parties (Carson *et al.* 2018, p. 3).

Beyond applications in the financial sector, blockchain applications are moving towards independent certification of product authenticity and quality or transparent certification of global supply management and more (White 2017).

Chapter 5

Digital Enterprise Software Solutions

Digital Enterprise Software and integration platforms are the base upon which various applications can be added to allow enterprises to create a single point of access to data across the enterprise. Modern IIoT platforms allow us to streamline all areas by creating a digital thread connecting previously unconnected elements and processes. Enterprise platforms have to support data and process integration from different software vendors across the extended enterprise and through the business of engineering, from the product lifecycle to all related technical and economical processes (Aras 2017, p. 12). The digital thread employs Digital Twins and enables asset visibility and management.

Digitization and the transformation of IIoT data into productive business results are core drivers. A clear structure is required to enable enterprises to connect assets to the cloud and to use the IIoT data (Siemens 2017g, p. 6). Due to the wide application span and complexity of the code, a single software vendor will not be able to offer every application that enterprises need. Some vendors offer open IIoT-platforms as a service which can be used as a foundation for software from other vendors when building a specific infrastructure for digital enterprises. Application programming interfaces (APIs) allow software developers to plug into other specific applications without having to know anything about the complex code inside those applications.

Following the digital thread, in the first phase of the digital enterprise concept the focus is on integrated product engineering. For this application area many tools are already available in the market. The second phase includes the plant design and optimization in a collaborative environment concurrently with the product engineering. At this level many tools are available for specific purposes but there is still a lack of integration and multi-criteria optimization. The third phase of the digital enterprise concept focuses on the operational production planning and control on the factory floor. This approach requires an extremely high effort and future research is needed to develop methods and tools for this approach.

5.1 Requirements

A Digital Enterprise Platform shall enable team collaboration to support interactions through all functions across all disciplines of an enterprise. This includes mechanical, software and electrical design, systems analysis, production and logistic planning and quality assurance across the extended enterprise with suppliers and partners. Both formal and informal collaboration is required. Formal collaboration is required for implementing engineering changes and establishing processes, rules and workflows that adhere and create an audit trail that records critical decisions. Informal collaboration covers unstructured communication when discussing design proposals, strategies, opportunities or problems.

Modern digital enterprises require a holistic approach to optimize the entire value chain by use of integrated software solutions in order to create a digital image of the entire value chain. Therefore, a comprehensive digital enterprise platform has to provide the technical foundation supporting all required digital transformations. A comprehensive software portfolio has to enable connections between people and processes with data and applications for real-time based decision-making. In order to form a smart innovation environment, real-time production information and smart virtual models have to be connected across the lifecycle phases and the value chain from ideation and planning up to realization. The idea is to digitalize an entire environment of products and plants and to realize the benefit of digitalization, including shorter time-to-market, improved production flexibility and significantly reduced costs.

The IIoT integration requires us to aggregate, analyze and transform the generated data for actionable information. These can be fed back to product development and production planning to create a completely closed loop decision environment for continuous optimization. Digital Enterprises have to close the loop through product ideation, realization and utilization to seamlessly integrate operational data throughout the value chain in order to drive operational efficiency. This can be achieved by running simulations and testing results with physical-world observations (Siemens 2018e).

Digital enterprise platforms are required to have the ability to manage data, which includes process and knowledge management. The product configuration from the concept through the entire lifecycle has to be managed and traceability forward and backwards provided. This requires the ability to provide services and sustainability, and the ability to support enterprise data and the process management requirements of upgradeability over a long period, at reasonable costs (CIMdata 2017a, p. 8).

Sustainability requires adaptability, extensibility and maintainability. Adaptability is the ability to configure data models, user interfaces and workflows to the need of specific enterprise requirements over time. Extensibility offers the possibility of extending the platform capabilities to expand core technology at any time and maintainability allows us to stay current with organizational, process and IT technology changes at reasonable cost. Unfortunately, sustainability is never easy to assess and requires continuous improvement to reach and keep at maturity (CIMdata 2017b, p. 5).

Digital enterprise platforms shall enable us to transform IIoT data into meaningful and actionable information for enterprises. This requires us to include actual and historical data from enterprise resource planning, manufacturing execution systems, supervisory control and data acquisition systems. A data-driven digital transformation requires robust and suitable data architecture with strong governance to enable activities such as interconnected objects, analytics, Artificial Intelligence and security (Atos 2018b). Digital enterprise solutions shall enable a seamless integration of operational data throughout the value chain and provide Digital Twins with analytics, simulation or Artificial Intelligence models in order to drive operational efficiency.

5.2 Platform Architecture

Digital enterprise architecture is related to information technology. But in addition to technology, it has also to cover aspects such as business operations, manufacturing or logistics, finance, people and buildings. An enterprise architect must understand these areas at least well enough to supervise the teams and specialists involved. For enterprise integration scenario openness is critical to facilitate the flexibility, speed and agility of further development as well as the long-term success and sustainability of IT systems. To enable the interoperability, portability and extensibility of at least the open interfaces, open data models and open architecture have to be applied to enable the integration of various devices and software not limited to specific vendors.

Future planning models will be much more dynamic and flexible, making the best use of machines and global capacity, responding to demand and opportunities. Factories will increasingly be part of a network and manufacturing will decouple from specific plants and software. Further activities will decouple from specific hardware. Each contributing facility should be comparable with others and benchmarked against central standards in order that they can learn from each other (Atos 2016, p. 10). Of course this requires changes for future enterprise architectures.

5.2.1 *Future Enterprise Architecture*

In digital enterprises the platform architecture is changing from the traditional ISA-95 manufacturing architecture (Fig. 5.1, left side) towards future designs considering IIoT connectivity, edge and cloud computing. Further digital modelling, applications and collaboration between processes and big data have to be considered. The design can be still applied on separate layers, as shown in Fig. 5.1, or even better, it can be changed from a layer structure to service oriented approaches as shown in Chapter 5.2.4. Future enterprise platforms require a high degree of flexibility and shall be scalable and adaptable. The communication and controls shall not be limited within the borders of a factory or single enterprise. Further, to react flexible to rapidly changing demands, modern production controls have to enable smart pull mechanisms. These mechanisms require an enterprise architecture that is very well connected and offers flexible real-time communication.

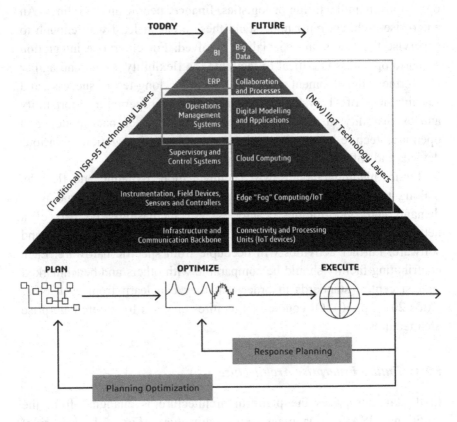

Fig. 5.1. Future Enterprise Architecture (Dassault Systèmes 2017b, p. 8).

In a next-generation model, enterprises use advanced technologies with digital models applying simulation and Artificial Intelligence to improve business operations. Modern enterprise platforms have to enable these and other upcoming technologies. To stay successful in the long run, the enterprise architecture has to offer the capability to evolve and adapt flexibly and quickly as business requirements change (Bollard *et al.* 2017, p. 5).

5.2.2 *Digital Stack*

Real-time access to data and devices is fundamentally driven by the continuous flow of information and action between the physical and digital world. This flow occurs through iterative loops including the following steps: physical-to-digital, digital-to-digital and digital-to-physical.

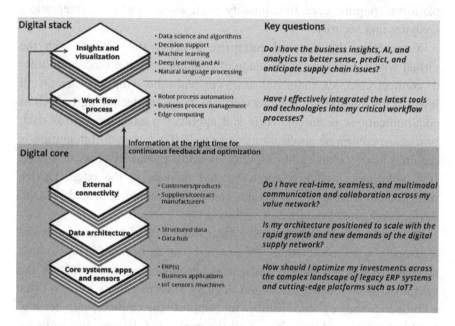

Fig. 5.2. The Digital Stack (Mussomeli *et al.* 2016, p. 14).

The digital core architecture provides a single place to access near-real-time network data and the digital stack (Fig. 5.2), includes multiple layers that synchronize and integrate these data to support and enable informed decision-making. This integrated digital stack supports a free flow of information across information clusters and provides a single location to access near real-time data from multiple sources such as products, customers, suppliers and aftermarket support encapsulating multiple perspectives (Mussomeli *et al.* 2016, p. 14).

5.2.3 *IIoT Connectivity*

For modern digital enterprise platforms IIoT connectivity is absolutely mandatory. IIoT platforms are software solutions that connect and manage smart devices and infrastructure in industrial and manufacturing environments to integrate operational data and control into business processes (Miller and Pelino 2018, pp. 2-3; Gartner 2018). IIoT platforms require core functionality such as connectivity, integration, analytics and security.

Connecting the physical enterprise systems and devices with the virtual world requires a wide range of communication protocols in order to connect complex industrial assets in real-time with software on all levels. This integration includes software, tools and technologies such as communications protocols. APIs and application adapters address data, processes, enterprise applications and the IIoT ecosystem. Integration is required across cloud and on-premises implementations for end-to-end IIoT solutions, including gateways and devices at the edge. Device management enables us to create, configure, troubleshoot and manage devices and gateways remotely and securely.

IIoT scenarios mostly involve large numbers of connected devices measuring state information. This requires us to manage, simplify and standardize the process of configuring, provisioning and initiating the operation of connected assets and devices. IIoT platforms have to offer a broad range of capabilities to support the monitoring, testing, troubleshooting and updating of all the connected devices and software involved. Data management includes capabilities that support gathering endpoint and edge device data, storing data from edge to enterprise platforms, providing data accessibility, data tracking and enforcing data and analytics governance policies to ensure the quality, security, privacy and currency of data.

Advanced analytics are increasingly important in IIoT platforms, including advanced analytics which use Artificial Intelligence to transform data into actionable insights. In digital enterprises many sensors capture and generate real-time data and audio and video sensors deliver rich media insight. Analytics includes the processing of data streams to provide insights into asset states by monitoring them, providing indicators and tracking patterns. A variety of techniques, such as rule engines, event stream processing, data visualization and machine learning can be applied.

IIoT platforms shall enable developers to easily create applications, business rules and data management capabilities based on connectivity, security and manageability to support relevant business processes. Application management includes software that enables business applications in any deployment model to analyze data and accomplish IIoT-related business functions. Platforms shall enable runtime management and Digital Twins. Further, the platforms shall support cloud scalability and reliability, and seamlessly and with agility ensure the deployment and delivery of solutions. IIoT platforms have to protect devices and data from attack and to secure sensitive information. Security is a mandatory function of software, tools and practices. It is necessary to facilitate, to audit and to ensure compliance, as well as to establish and execute preventive, detective and corrective controls and actions to ensure privacy and the security of data across the enterprise.

5.2.4 *From Layers to Service Orientation*

Traditionally, enterprise architecture has been focusing on layering software systems, which are based on technology concerns such as data access, business logic, application logic and presentation logic. The benefits of a layering architecture are that modularity changes in one layer do not impact other layers and that standardization is limiting technology risks and leveraging economies of scales.

Compared to a layering architecture, a Domain-Driven-Design (DDD) with a set of loosely-coupled services is much more flexible. The domain is decomposed into sub-domains and contexts. The resulting domain architecture defines a set of loosely coupled services that encapsulate a set of homogenous capabilities. This architecture is based on the modularity rule that within a service cohesion is high, inter-service coupling is low and implementation details are hidden behind APIs. Each service owns its persistence mechanisms and exposes its functions and features through defined interfaces. Inter-service communication occurs through synchronous or asynchronous interactions. When communication is asynchronous, messages or events link services through protocols. In this approach no communication should be allowed through database sharing, shared libraries or other mechanisms.

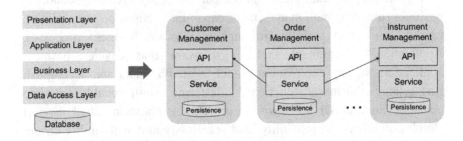

Fig. 5.3. From Layers to Services (Barbazange *et al*. 2018, p. 8).

With this approach the choice of tools and development stack is not constrained and teams are free to choose the tools to use. Services can be containerized, tested and deployed in isolation. Further innovation is not slowed down by technology standards that are likely to become obsolete over time. However, decomposing a domain requires deep domain knowledge to avoid design problems due to abstraction leaks (Barbazange *et al*. 2018, p. 8).

5.2.5 *Delivery as a service*

Platform suppliers increasingly offer systems in the form of a platform-as-a-service (PaaS) or a software-as-a-service (SaaS), delivering the use of integrated services through an Internet connection. This style of delivery allows customers to rent virtualized servers and associated services used to run existing applications. These can be applications including a variety of services and service combinations spanning the application development lifecycle. With the cloud-managed infrastructure, companies do not have to implement their own platform facilities but can take affordable advantage of the infinitely scalable computing capacity, which can be adapted to the demand of the particular digital enterprise. The platform can automatically be scaled to the required data volumes and the numbers of connected assets and users. The software supplier can implement a flexible cost model with on-demand flexibility and pay-per-use pricing (Siemens 2018f).

5.2.6 *Agile Architecture Frameworks*

Agility is an important issue and industrial enterprises have to become increasingly agile. Due to the fast changing demands of the market or global supply networks, technology changes and disruptions, the digital enterprises have to react quickly and flexibly. Agile enterprises regularly rethink and redesign their structures, mechanisms and processes to strike a balance between speed and stability.

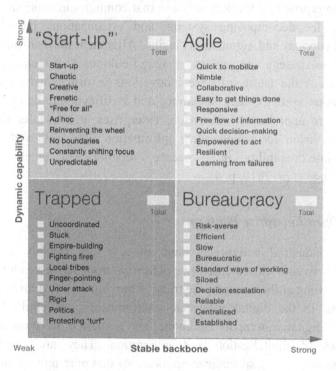

Fig. 5.4. Where does an Enterprise fall (Aghina *et al*. 2015, p. 3)?

Figure 5.4 gives a brief idea of how to check if an enterprise is already moving towards becoming an agile enterprise. This is based on placing check marks by every word that describes how it currently feels to work at the particular enterprise. The total number checked in each quadrant gives a first rough idea of where the enterprise is located regarding agility.

The pre-requisites of agility are agile processes and an agile architecture. While agile enterprises share a few behavioral norms, such as a bias for action and the free flow of information, other norms vary according to the nature of the enterprise and the specific approaches adopted to encourage a healthy, high-performing culture. A clearer and widely adopted open behavior throughout all levels and units of an enterprise enables it to change structures, governance and processes in pursuit of agility (Aghina *et al.* 2015, p. 12).

An Agile Architecture Framework (AAF) can meet the needs of the digital enterprises. It develops a vision that combines in a unique manner methods for decomposing systems and organizations into loosely-coupled services and autonomous teams. Alignment mechanisms rooted in business strategy can promote a shared culture. Architecture patterns can leverage the latest software innovations in distributed computing, autonomous systems, data streaming and Artificial Intelligence. Agile architecture approaches will enable enterprises at all scales to better realize a vision for boundaryless information flow, achieved through global interoperability in a secure, reliable and timely manner (Barbazange *et al.* 2018, p. 4).

5.2.7 *Open Enterprise Platforms*

Modern industrial enterprises have to act very flexibly in global networks. Even if closed enterprise platforms from single vendors might be very strong at the moment, the trend is moving very fast towards open solutions. In the digital enterprise environment open platforms as a scalable digital enterprise backbone are requested to transform the processes of digitalization and integration. They are required to independently create specialized applications that plug into an integrated digital enterprise environment and offer a fully mature, open and integrated environment. Open platforms have to enable robust applications using IIoT connectivity, advanced analytics and services, including data management, predictive learning and visualization to accelerate all processes.

Modern software platforms can be built on model-based Service-Oriented Architecture (SOA) which offer applications and core services that are inherently separate. This type of architecture allows the applications to be customized, extended and maintained. For enterprise systems, the Code of PLM Openness (CPO) is establishing a common understanding of the openness of IT systems in the context of PLM between IT, customers, vendors and service providers. The CPO also combines business with IT requirements and is a vehicle for establishing transparency with regard to openness, defining measurable criteria for interoperability, infrastructure, extensibility, interfaces, standards, architecture and partnership (ProSTEP iViP 2015).

The trend is moving towards open platforms with global IIoT connectivity, including application development with native cloud accessibility, delivered through software or platforms as a service. Open platforms are also a prerequisite for the success of AI applications. Enterprises cannot afford the constraints, limitations and costs which result from binding AI initiatives to a single technology platform (Atos 2018a, p. 6). Platforms without the ability to integrate any sensor, any device or any software from various vendors will not have a future chance in the long run.

5.3 Industrial Enterprise Platforms

Digital Enterprise Platforms build the technical software foundation of a digital enterprise. A Platform shall enable continuous integration from product development to product performance up to production and logistics operations. It has to support the automation of business from shop floor to top floor, allowing for the rapid development and validation of products and operations by creating Digital Twins. The platform shall enable an open and collaborative environment for managing a traceable digital thread between all platform processes and participants (Siemens 2018f).

Digital Enterprise Platforms are becoming a central focus and a key enabler for IIoT communication and a critical hub for the incorporation of key emerging technologies. Digital enterprise platforms built the software foundation of the digital enterprise and provide a platform for frameworks supporting the integration or collaboration between applications such as Product Lifecycle Management (PLM), Design Automation (DA), Product Data Management (PDM), Enterprise Resource Planning (ERP), Manufacturing Operations Management (MOM), Manufacturing Execution Systems (MES), Totally Integrated Automation (TIA), Asset Performance Management (APM), Application Lifecycle Management (ALM), Customer Relationship Management (CRM) and others.

An important subset of Digital Enterprise Platforms are IIoT-platforms, which are software solutions that connect and manage smart devices and infrastructure in industrial and manufacturing environments to integrate operational data and control into business processes. The cloud integration market is emerging with a large number of vendors and the role of integration technology and its implications is moving forward. Therefore, it is not trivial to consider solutions for future demands. Available on the market are enterprise integration platforms as a service. These address IIoT integration and API management capabilities including a variety of scenarios, such as application and data integration, processes and AI-enabled systems. There are some IIOT-cloud platform vendors that offer only an integration platform without specific industrial applications or solutions. These platforms can be used from others as a foundation to build specific solutions. Software as a service vendors often bundle cloud integration capabilities within existing products to integrate with third-party applications. Pure API management vendors do not provide integration capabilities within the appropriate layer of the digital architecture. Open Source Software tools reduce the license costs of software but increase the consulting costs that go along with more hands-on-coding and specialized skills.

IIoT platforms have been evaluated by the Forrester Report, Q3 2018 (Miller and Pelino 2018). This report identifies providers such as Amazon Web Services (AWS), Atos, Bosch, C3 IoT, Cisco, GE Digital, Hitachi, IBM, Microsoft, Oracle, PTC, SAP, Schneider Electric, Siemens and Software AG.

Industrial application-related digital enterprise platforms, available for industrial solutions, are platforms such as Aras Innovator, Autodesk Fusion, Dassault Systems 3DEXPERIENCE, General Electric Predix, IBM Open Integrated Systems Approach, Oracle Cloud Platform, PTC ThingWorx IoT-Platform, Siemens Digital Innovation Platform, SAP HANA Cloud Platform and others. Not all of these cover all industrial areas and applications. Due to the focus and size of the enterprise, the customer has to specify his requirements and decide what fits best with his particular demand.

Some vendors offer more than one solution, partly a well-settled solution with many licenses in the market and additionally a new cloud-based approach, which is new in the market. Due to their future relevance, in the following the focus is always on the new, innovative and advanced approaches, even if these may be not widespread at the time being. Increasingly, many software vendors are building strategic partnerships with one or more IIoT cloud platform vendors (such as Amazon Web Services, Google or Microsoft Azure), which will become the primary platforms for building and deploying specific services and the business logic on which these vendors run their particular businesses (SoftwareAG 2018a, p. 3).

The following section gives a brief introduction to the platforms and related software available in the marked. The information about available platforms is listed in alphabetic order of the vendors. Due to the rapid changes in the software market this information cannot cover all software vendors and solutions and the presented information is based on input from the particular vendors and shows a snapshot from the year 2018. Technologies and software are still changing rapidly. Actual and more detailed information about tools and solutions are available on the internet pages of the particular software and system vendors.

5.3.1 *Aras - Innovator Platform*

The Aras Innovator platform allows us to manage the lifecycle of complex multi-disciplinary products including requirements, development, manufacturing and support. It integrates applications that support PDM, PLM and more into a single platform. Aras uses an open source business model and an agile software solution that can quickly adapt to specific requirements (Fleming 2017, p. 9).

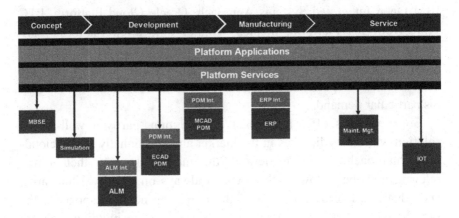

Fig. 5.5. Aras Platform Integration (Aras 2018b, p. 8).

The core architecture of the Aras PLM Platform is a service-oriented architecture (SOA) that separates applications from underlying services. Applications are built and modified with the Aras modeling engine using the services required for the particular application. Because Aras is built around open standards, it is relatively easy to integrate information with other business systems and data models.

Aras is coming from the PLM side into the digital enterprise platform market and has pre-built applications that span the lifecycle from requirements management to technical documentation. The product engineering application helps to define and manage information throughout the product lifecycle from design and development, verification and validation, manufacturing and service, to the end of the life cycle. The program management application automates the product development process with comprehensive tools for monitoring projects and managing new product development. The requirements management application supports systems engineering by providing an enterprise-wide, multidisciplinary platform for managing physical, functional, logical and performance-related requirements that can be linked to specifications, parts, BOMs, test plans or other objects. The component engineering enables us to select, source and compare the electronic components that best meet the requirements. The quality management application provides organizations with advanced product quality planning. Failure mode effects analysis tools offer to manage risk, improve quality and attain environmental, regulatory, safety, medical and other forms of compliance.

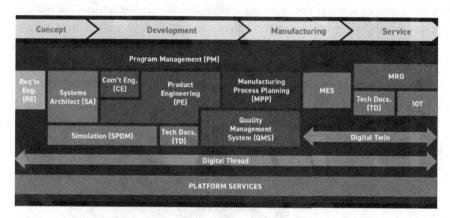

Fig. 5.6. ARAS Application Span (Aras 2018b, p. 9).

The basic applications for product engineering and program management are bundled with Aras Innovator and contain the fundamental open-access capabilities of the solution. Remaining applications, such as requirements management, component engineering, technical documents, quality management and other enhanced capabilities are available via subscription. As an open source provider, Aras hosts an online community for customers to share ideas and innovations and open-access, non-commercial community projects. Partners are developing industry-specific solutions and expansions (Aras 2018b). Further, Aras and IBM have established a strategic partnership and are working together to enable clients to manage the full digital thread and Digital Twin across engineering, manufacturing, operations and maintenance.

5.3.2 *Autodesk - Fusion Platform*

Autodesk has a strong background in design and simulation software such as AutoCAD and focuses on small and medium size customers. With the Fusion platform, Autodesk offers a SaaS deployment approach, which integrates the product development processes and product lifecycle management using connected cloud-based production processes. The flexible cloud infrastructure allows us to connect enterprises, supply chains and customers for ongoing collaboration. Fusion unifies the design process, allowing us to conceptualize, design and test ideas in a single environment and to build a bridge from design to manufacturing. Autodesk is moving towards the demand for more flexible manufacturing processes and is beginning to drive industrial additive manufacturing (Fleming 2017, p. 11).

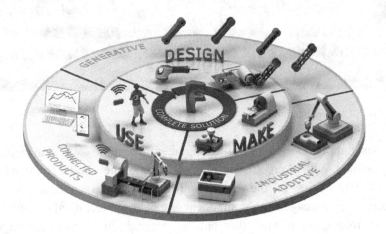

Fig. 5.7. Autodesk Fusion Platform (Autodesk 2016, p. 4).

Fusion 360 is a cloud-based 3D CAD, CAM and CAE platform. With the Manufacturing 3D printing utility Slice, building supports and generating toolpaths for a variety of 3D printers are possible. CNC lathe machines with traditional toolpaths such as facing, roughing, grooving, drilling and more can be programed. The water jet, laser cutter and plasma cutter features allow us to create efficient multi-axis toolpaths with collision control for complex 3D designs. With the nonlinear stress module, permanent deformations and nonlinear materials can be analyzed using cloud simulation and with the cloud based event simulation the dynamic behavior can be investigated (Autodesk 2018a).

Fusion Lifecycle offers product lifecycle management capabilities and improves team coordination and productivity. Fusion Production combines production management features including scheduling, job tracking and machine monitoring using IIoT cloud computing. It is possible to create work instructions, dispatch job sheets, schedule tasks, track jobs, monitor workstations and view performance reports.

Fusion Production gives design, manufacturing and operations teams real-time visibility and instant access to production data in a single, cloud-based tool. It enables smart manufacturing and uses data-driven insights about production performance (Autodesk 2018b).

5.3.3 *Atos – Codex Platform*

Atos, a global company in digital transformation, offers in Atos Codex a portfolio of services and products designed to accelerate and industrialize the enterprise adoption of data analytics and related activities central to digital transformation strategies (Atos 2018c). The platform spans IIoT connectivity, data analytics, AI, deep learning, machine learning and cognitive computing. Atos Codex AI Suite is an application toolset for cognitive capabilities, providing the tools needed to scope, develop, roll-out and manage AI applications. AI applications created and managed with Atos Codex AI Suite are platform-independent. Atos offers platform solutions through Codex IoT built on their own infrastructure. In order to deliver the most advanced use cases in multiple environments, Atos leverages Atos Codex AI Suite and Google Cloud Platform.

Further, Atos has public cloud partnerships with AWS and Microsoft Azure and also provides development, hosting and integration services to Siemens MindSphere customers (Miller and Pelino 2018, p. 14).

5.3.4 *Amazon - Web Services (AWS)*

AWS offers cloud computing to build innovative solutions and migrate critical applications and the shift to the cloud helps enterprises to transform businesses, gain agility and improve operational responsiveness. The IoT platform solutions from AWS offer analytics, device management and edge services. Customers can use the IoT services on the AWS Cloud to access a range of cloud-based capabilities, including data storage, processing and analytics. AWS provides enterprises with a portfolio of over 120 services, including cutting edge technologies and reliable cloud infrastructure, making applications globally available without compromising capacity or security. AWS offers a global and diverse ecosystem of partners and a dynamic community of professional services, enterprise support offerings and solutions architects in the cloud (Anon. 2018).

AWS IoT Core is a managed cloud platform connecting devices securely with cloud applications and other devices. The AWS IoT Core enables us to continuously ingest, filter, transform and route the data streamed from connected devices and take actions based on the data and route it for further processing and analytics (AWS 2018a).

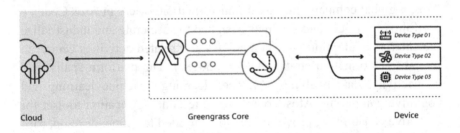

Fig. 5.8. AWS Greengrass (Amazon Web Services 2018).

AWS Greengrass runs at the edge and offers messaging, data caching, sync and ML inference capabilities on connected devices in a secure way. Devices connected with Greengrass can run AWS Lambda functions, execute predictions based on machine learning models, keep device data in sync, communicate with other devices securely and transmit necessary information back to the cloud. Greengrass devices can act locally at the edge on the data generated in order to respond quickly to local events, while still using the cloud for management, analytics and durable storage. Greengrass uses the same security and access management as the IoT Core, with mutual device authentication, authorization and secure connectivity to the cloud. Greengrass enables us to build IoT solutions that connect different types of devices with the cloud and each other (Amazon Web Services 2018).

AWS IoT Analytics is a fully-managed IoT analytics service, fully integrated with AWS IoT Core, that collects, pre-processes, enriches, stores and analyzes IoT device data at scale. IoT Analytics can perform simple ad hoc queries as well as complex analysis and it is a possibility to run IoT analytics in order to understand the performance of devices, predicting device failures and machine learning (AWS 2018b).

AWS provides customers with a horizontal platform and a wide range of database, analytics and storage services. It lets customers address these generic functions at scale. This platform has only a very few industrially-focused prebuilt applications but it offers a very comprehensive general solution and is used in hosting other industrial IoT software platforms (Miller and Pelino 2018, p. 15).

5.3.5 *Cisco – Jasper Platform*

Cisco offers in Jasper a global IoT platform for launching and managing connected IoT services to drive business transformation in order to automate connectivity management with embedded connectivity and networks for devices to connect to through applications (Cisco 2017). The Jasper Control Center provides set and forget automation of the entire IoT service lifecycle and offers a real-time network with continuous monitoring of changing network conditions and device behavior. Jasper is deeply integrated into numerous operator groups globally.

Jasper provides limited support for industrial applications and Digital Twin functionality (Miller and Pelino 2018), but it is an IOT platform which can be used as a base to set up specific application-based enterprise functionality for industrial IoT use cases.

5.3.6 *Constellation Research - C3 Platform*

C3 delivers a comprehensive platform-as-a-service (PaaS) for rapidly developing and operating big data, Artificial Intelligence and IoT software-as-a-service (SaaS) applications, including a family of configurable and extensible SaaS products developed with and operating on its PaaS. The C3 Platform is an integrated family of software engineering and administration tools for designing, developing, deploying and operating big data, predictive analytics and IoT SaaS applications.

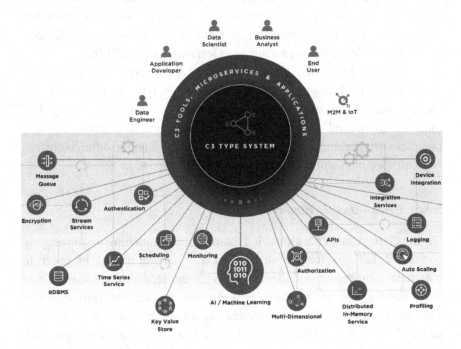

Fig. 5.9. C3 Platform (C3 2018b).

The platform is a data object-centric abstraction layer that binds the various components, including infrastructure and services. It enables the deployment of Software-as-a-Service (SaaS) applications that integrate and process dynamic data sets from sensor networks, industrial equipment and other information systems. The platform applies predictive analytics, data exploration and Artificial Intelligence intended to enable companies to build next generation enterprise applications (C3 2018a; C3 2018b).

The platform (Fig. 5.9) integrates production data from independent data sources and sensors aggregated using scalable computation and storage architectures. The sensor health module ensures the deployment and operational health of IoT sensor devices and the predictive maintenance module helps to predict, diagnose and reduce equipment or system failures. The inventory optimization module focuses on reducing inventory costs and improving cash flow while lowering the risk of stock-outs. The supply network module helps to evaluate supply network patterns in suppliers, production facilities and logistics. The CRM module helps to identify revenue opportunities, predict and prevent problems and enable efficient service delivery and the energy management module focuses on energy asset lifecycle management.

The platform is used to develop AI-centric enterprise applications that use real-time data correlated with operational system data to deliver predictive maintenance, detection of loss/fraud and sensor network health management. The platform is a fully integrated production platform for designing, developing, deploying, provisioning and managing industrial scale AI, big data, predictive analytic and IoT applications. It leverages Artificial Intelligence and the cloud to aggregate all type of data into a unified, federated cloud image for analysis (C3 2018a).

5.3.7 *Dassault Systems - 3DEXPERIENCE Platform*

Dassault Systems offers in the DELMIA 3DEXPERIENCE platform (Fig. 5.10) a collaborative digital enterprise platform which can provide digital continuity through the enterprise from marketing and sales to engineering. Dassault Systems focuses the platform on digital manufacturing and drives manufacturing innovation and efficiency by planning, simulating and modeling global production processes. It shall enable manufacturers to create digital models that virtually simulate products, processes and factory operations. The solution is designed to support the unique requirements of assembly operators in complex assembly manufacturing environments such as aerospace or industrial equipment. An integral part of the platform is the connection made between the virtual and physical worlds to drive global decision support with real-time visibility and predictive analysis (Dassault Systèmes 2017a).

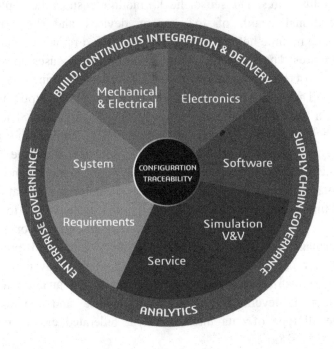

Fig. 5.10. Dassault Systems 3DEXPERIENCE Platform (Dassault Systèmes 2018, p. 14).

The DELMIA 3DEXPERIENCE Platform enables manufacturers to create digital models that virtually simulate products, processes and factory operations. Software modules cover the areas of additive manufacturing, ergonomics, lean manufacturing, machining, manufacturing operations management, process engineering, robotics and virtual factory. Additive manufacturing offers modules to drive manufacturing innovation and efficiency with tools to support planning, simulating and programming additive manufacturing processes. Ergonomics includes tools assessing working conditions, ensuring compliance and verifying assembly across multiple platforms. Lean manufacturing enables manufacturers to make lean practices an integral part of shop floor operations. Machining offers tools for defining the behavior of programmable CNC machines. Manufacturing operations management modules help manufacturers to transform global production operations to achieve and sustain operational excellence. Process engineering includes tools to create and optimize build-to-order and lean production manufacturing systems. Robotics offers tools performing reachability studies, interlock analysis and offline robot teaching to deliver optimized robotics programs to the shop floor. Virtual factory provides solutions for the creation and simulation of a 3D Digital Twin of the factory (Dassault Systèmes 2018).

The platform allows end-to-end management for the development, planning and simulation of hardware and software regarding mechanical, electrical and electronic software and services. The platform gives access to various DELMIA tools such as CATIA for design, SOLIDWORKS for design in manufacturing, ENOVIA for product lifecycle management, SIMULIA for realistic simulation applications, EXALEAD for data in business solutions and BIOVIA for providing global, collaborative product lifecycle experiences to transform scientific innovation capabilities (Dassault Systèmes 2017a).

5.3.8 *General Electric - Predix Platform*

GE offers in the Predix Platform a distributed application and services platform for building and running digital industrial solutions delivering multiple outcomes across various industries. Scheduling and logistics increase asset utilization with predictive analytics improving performance and efficiency. Connected products replace fixed models with a predict and prevent service approach in order to collect and analyze data. Field service management gives workers the machine data, expertise and processes to schedule work orders to improve repairs and upgrades. Industrial analytics monitors asset health to identify problems using predictive and prescriptive analytics to boost productivity. Asset performance management achieves new levels of performance, reliability and availability throughout the life cycle of assets. Operations optimization uses key insights on an enterprise-wide scaling to resolve operational issues driving productivity and increasing efficiencies (General Electric 2018c, p. 9).

Key elements of the Predix cloud include scalable, public cloud infrastructure abstraction and automation. The Predix Platform services can be executed across edge and cloud to optimize workload execution. The platform offers a comprehensive software portfolio integrating traditional enterprise IT solutions with a native architecture that augments industrial operational technologies for GE and non-GE assets. Predix is built for large-scale machine data processing, data management and analytics. It offers services in the following categories: industrial services (Asset Services, Modeling), data services (Time Series Data, Modern Hadoop Database, Data Lakes), analytics services (Catalog, Orchestration, Execution), security services (User Account and Authentication, Access Control Service) and software configuration services (Miller and Pelino 2018, p. 14).

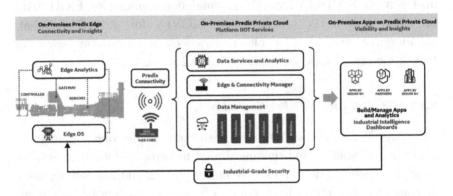

Fig. 5.11. GE Predix Platform (General Electric 2018c, p. 7).

Predix Manufacturing Execution Systems (MES) is a suite of solutions that can transform a manufacturing business through insights and intelligence powered by data integration, IIoT, machine learning and predictive analytics (General Electric 2018d). The Predix Platform is built around an asset-centric Digital Twin, creating actionable insights from asset data and analytics. It provides a comprehensive edge-to-cloud architecture that optimizes workloads across varying operating infrastructures and supports control and productivity development. The platform runs SaaS applications such as Predix Asset Performance Management (Predix APM), which increases asset reliability and availability. The Predix platform equips industrial organizations to rapidly build, securely deploy and effectively run IIoT applications from edge to cloud, turning asset data into actionable insights (General Electric 2018c, p. 4).

The platform includes cloud and edge technology stacks that work together to support complex, distributed applications. Analytics asset connectivity and management allow us to collect, process and securely transfer data from assets to analytics and applications in the cloud. Digital twins are software-based dynamic digital representations of physical assets and systems which take advantage of industrial-grade analytics to model and optimize physical-word assets. Analytics and machine learning are used to improve analytics capabilities, generating insights across the entire life cycle of industrial assets. Big data processing offers options for ingestion, analytics execution and storage for streaming and processing. Stringent security measures are designed into the fabric of the platform, forming a continuously monitored, protected platform with which operators and developers can secure industrial innovation. Application development environments support productivity and control (General Electric 2018c, pp. 7-8).

5.3.9 *Hitachi – Lumada Platform*

Hitachi Vantara offers in the Lumada IoT Platform a framework that aims to accelerate IoT solution creation. The Platform includes modules which provide an end-to-end view that addresses the edge-to-analytics needs for any IoT deployment. The Lumada IoT platform collects, blends, analyses and acts on human, machine and business data from across the enterprise (Hitachi 2018).

Lumada Edge extracts, filters, analyzes and executes rules on data generated on edge for a comprehensive, real-time view of the asset status. Lumada Core integrates, manages, monitors and collects data of various types using fast and scalable APIs to extract information for analysis and to map information to physical assets in the form of asset avatars (Digital Twins).

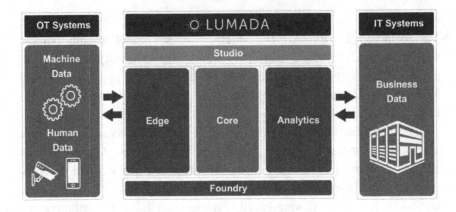

Fig. 5.12. Hitachi Lumada Platform (Hitachi 2018).

Lumada Analytics brings together data analytics, machine learning, Artificial Intelligence and a range of advanced algorithms to operate on the IoT data pipelines to continually increase optimization and allow organizations to make real-time informed decisions. Lumada Studio includes analytic information, alerts and notifications and widgets to implement application logic for fast, meaningful insights into data and devices. Lumada Foundry delivers security services and technologies to build, package, deploy, scale and manage microservice applications on-premises or in the cloud (MacGillivray 2018). Hitachi focuses on the Digital Twin, which it refers to as an asset avatar (Miller and Pelino 2018, p. 13).

5.3.10 *IBM - Open Integrated Systems Approach*

IBM is running a continuous engineering approach with platform components and solutions to capture and manage requirements and traceability to other engineering artifacts (Fig. 5.13). IBM offers a full-stack cloud platform that spans public, private and hybrid environments. The Cloud offers ways to migrate, modernize, build and connect cloud applications by moving and managing workloads across clouds with an open container architecture. Workload migration techniques ease the transition to the cloud and allow us to innovate and modernize apps on a globally available public or private cloud platform.

IBM is strong in predictive analytics and machine learning. IBM builds its IIoT-platform on extensive analytics with industry-specific and services expertise. The platform offers a comprehensive array of capabilities, including augmented reality, cognitive data processing, blockchain, edge analytics and natural language processing. IBM favors its own cloud, offering a limited set of public, private and on-premises delivery options. IBM has created a set of out-of-the-box solutions, such as prescriptive maintenance, that incorporate common equipment types and specialized manufacturing analytics (Miller and Pelino 2018, p. 11).

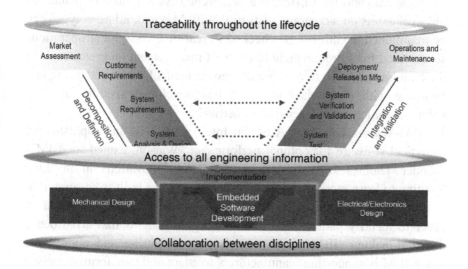

Fig. 5.13. IBM Open Integrated Systems Approach (Mayer 2017, p. 8).

IBM IoT Continuous Engineering is a group of five IBM products that cover the systems and software development lifecycle. IBM Rational DOORS Next Generation is a scalable product to optimize communication, collaboration and verification of requirements. IBM Rational Rhapsody products offer proven modeling and design activities. IBM Rational Quality Manager is a collaborative, web-based, quality management product that offers comprehensive test planning and test asset management from requirements to defects. IBM Rational Team Concert manages plans, tasks and project statuses as the critical link between required and delivered work. IBM Rational Engineering Lifecycle Manager helps us to visualize, analyze and gain insight from engineering lifecycle data. These products help teams to manage the complexity of developing smart, connected products (IBM 2018a). The IBM Rational Collaborative Lifecycle Management Solution is a set of seamlessly integrated application lifecycle management (ALM) tools that work together as one. Collaborative Lifecycle Management (CLM) can be used to manage requirements, plan projects, track changes and manage quality, all on a single platform.

What Maximo IBM offers is a comprehensive solution for managing physical assets on a common platform. With Maximo, all asset types can be maintained, health can be checked in real-time and global operations streamlined from procurement to contract management on premises or in the cloud. In addition to meeting the requirements for manufacturing and facilities with core Maximo, IBM has developed specific industry solutions for key asset-intensive industries.

IBM-Watson combines Artificial Intelligence (AI) and sophisticated analytical software for optimal performance. Watson, named for IBM's founder Thomas J. Watson, uses the latest innovations in machine learning to learn more with less data. Models can be built from scratch or existing APIs and pre-trained business solutions can be leveraged in order to identify patterns and trends and gain insights that drive better decision-making (IBM 2018b). In the manufacturing and operational space IBM is supporting manufacturers to adapt and transform processes through the IBM Watson IIoT platform. The approach leverages the existing infrastructure, physical equipment, systems and applications, using powerful accelerators (IBM 2017c, p. 4).

Jazz is IBM's initiative to transform software and systems delivery into open, collaborative services. Unlike the monolithic, closed products of the past, Jazz is an open platform designed to support industry participants in improving the software lifecycle and in breaking down walls between tools. It includes IoT Continuous Engineering, Collaborative Lifecycle Management, Rational DOORS Next Generation, Rational Team Concert, Rational Quality Manager, Rational Engineering Lifecycle Manager, Rational Publishing Engine, Jazz

Reporting Service, Rhapsody Model Manager, Rational Team Concert for agile teams and Enterprise Scaled Agile Framework (IBM 2018c).

5.3.11 *Microsoft - Azure Platform*

Microsoft provides in Azure a cloud platform that includes a set of cloud services to manage applications on a global network using diverse tools and frameworks in order to increase efficiency and productivity.

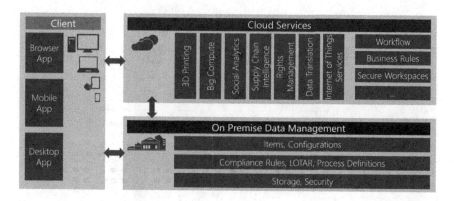

Fig. 5.14. Microsoft Azure Hybrid Platform (Microsoft 2018, p. 64).

The platform enables us to establish security, compliance and privacy requirements for enterprises, consistently meeting a broad set of international and industry-specific compliance standards and rigorous third-party audits to adhere to strict security controls and mandates. Due to the demand from customers who do not want to run everything in a public cloud, Azure and Azure Stack provide a way to run the same applications even in an on-premises environment (Fig. 5.14).

Microsoft does not have a focus on prebuilt applications for industrial use cases. Microsoft offers enabling cloud infrastructure, a comprehensive set of development tools and a rich set of advanced analytics capabilities. It continues to invest in end-to-end security and in releasing an increasingly broad set of open source tools. The public cloud infrastructure is used by many industrial IoT software platforms as a base for their specific enterprise platforms (Miller and Pelino 2018, p. 12).

5.3.12 *Oracle - Cloud Platform*

The Oracle Cloud Platform is a comprehensive, standards-based combination of Oracle-specific and open source technologies to enable us to efficiently build, deploy, integrate, secure and manage enterprise applications.

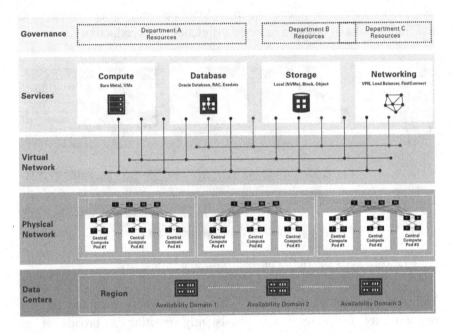

Fig. 5.15. Oracle Cloud Infrastructure and Architecture (Rahi 2017, p. 7).

Leveraging Artificial Intelligence and machine learning, Oracle provides autonomous PaaS solutions that are self-driving, self-securing and self-repairing, helping enterprises to innovate faster, make smarter decisions and deliver exceptional customer experience.

The Oracle Cloud Platform is optimized for hybrid and multi-cloud environments offering integrated IIoT applications on a scalable platform-as-a-service (PaaS) (Miller and Pelino 2018, p. 14). The integrated PaaS solution is offering three primary cloud services. The Internet of Things Cloud Service builds and deploys applications that can capture and analyze IoT data. The Big Data Cloud Service automates a high-powered cloud environment that has been designed to advance existing analytical capabilities. The Big Data Discovery Cloud Service runs on the Big Data Cloud Service and securely runs a wide range of big data workloads (Oracle 2016a).

The cloud infrastructure combines the flexibility and utility of a public cloud with the granular control, security and predictability of on-premises infrastructure (Rahi 2017, p. 2). In this cloud infrastructure Oracle offers cloud applications with adaptive intelligence which have built in the ability to update and maintain the various machine learning models automatically. These applications include an IoT cloud service, a customer experience cloud (Oracle CX Cloud), a human capital management cloud (Oracle HCM Cloud), a supply chain management cloud (Oracle SCM Cloud), an enterprise resource planning cloud (Oracle ERP Cloud) and an enterprise performance management cloud (Oracle EPM Cloud). These applications use data from the Oracle Data Cloud to supplement the data collected and generated within the applications. The cloud platform is available within the data center managed by Oracle (Tierney 2017).

5.3.13 *PTC - ThingWorx IoT-Platform*

PTC is a global software company delivering in ThingWorx a technology platform that can design, manufacture, operate and service things for a smart, connected world. The platform is delivering software in the fields of computer-aided design, product lifecycle management, software solutions for service, augmented reality for enterprises and engineering mathematical software. It works well with products such as Windchill (PLM) and Creo (CAD). With the ThingWorx IoT-Platform, PTC offers a single IoT solution for all industrial automation data. ThingWorx Industrial Connectivity connects disparate automation devices and software applications, enabling enterprises to derive the benefits from the Industrial Internet of Things. The platform leverages OPC and IT-centric communication protocols to provide a single source of industrial automation data to enterprise applications. With a library of many device drivers, client drivers and advanced plug-ins, the platform enables connectivity to many devices and other data sources, providing visibility across the enterprise for improved decision-making from the shop floor to the top floor (PTC 2017).

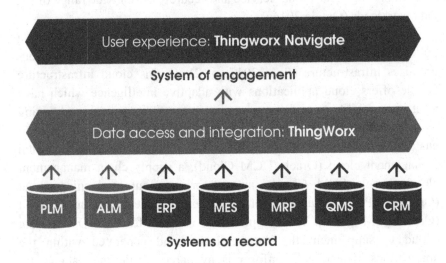

Fig. 5.16. ThingWorx Platform (PTC 2017, p. 4).

The platform connects Augmented Reality (AR), Extended Product Lifecycle Management (ePLM), Application Lifecycle Management (ALM), Service Lifecycle Management (SLM) and Computer-Aided Design (CAD) with all levels of the enterprise (PTC 2017).

5.3.14 *Siemens - Digital Innovation Platform*

Siemens has a strong engineering background and offers in the Digital Innovation Platform a broad technical software foundation for digital enterprise applications. The platform, which includes Teamcenter, MindSphere, Tia-Portal and others, is supporting product development, product performance and production operations. The platform includes an integrated portfolio of enterprise software and industrial automation solutions, which apply a holistic approach to optimize the entire value chain, in order to enable manufacturing companies to integrate and digitalize the business processes, including the processes of the suppliers.

The flow of information between all platform ecosystem participants creates a traceable digital thread and enables an open and collaborative environment. The solutions are available for discrete and process industries (Siemens 2018f).

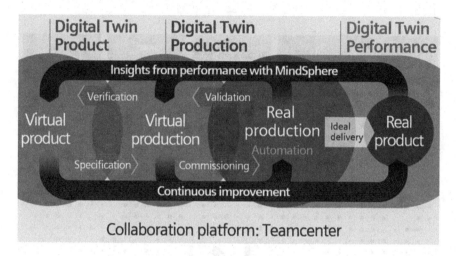

Fig. 5.17. Closed Loop Product Optimization (Siemens 2018f).

The Digital Enterprise Suite is built on a platform framework supporting collaboration, open IIoT, 3D-modeling and manufacturing operations. Supported applications are mechanical design, electronic design automation, software delivery, simulation and test, manufacturing planning, factory automation, manufacturing operations, performance and analytics. The suite integrates Product Lifecycle Management (PLM), Manufacturing Operations Management (MOM) and Totally Integrated Automation (TIA) which are based on the collaboration platform Teamcenter. Through the cloud-based open IoT operating system MindSphere IIoT devices can be connected.

Siemens offers in MindSphere a cloud-based open IIoT operating system that connects products, plants, systems, machines, enterprise applications and legacy databases with a secure plug-and-play connection. As part of a complete digitalization strategy, MindSphere enables powerful digital services and industry applications including Digital Twins. It is also possible to connect third-party products and industrial devices to the platform (Siemens 2018l). Building on their industrial strength, Siemens also delivers a range of hardware devices for deployment at the edge and further prebuilt applications for end users are available (Miller and Pelino 2018, p. 14).

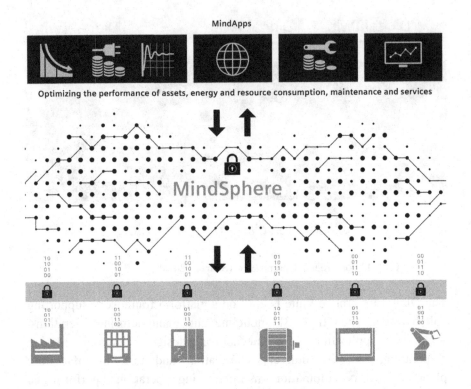

Fig. 5.18. Siemens MindSphere IIot-Platform (Siemens 2018l, p. 2).

The Totally Integrated Automation Portal (TIA Portal) as part of the Digital Enterprise Software Suite is the gateway to automation in the Digital Enterprise. The TIA Portal provides access to the digitalized automation services, from digital planning and integrated engineering to transparent operation. It allows enterprises to create projects using software generators and reducing the number of redundant workflows. With Teamcenter, the planning, engineering and design aspects of projects can be managed and merged (Siemens 2017g).

With an open platform-as-a-service approach Siemens is creating a partner ecosystem with domain-specific industry applications, digital services and closed-loop innovation with complete Digital Twins enabled (Siemens 2017g, p. 10). Siemens is actively encouraging a growing community of third-party developers and partners onto the platform and has set up worldwide application centers for digital customer applications in the industrial sector (Siemens 2018e). Domain expertise across industries and the global scale of Amazon Web Services (AWS) and Microsoft Azure public cloud infrastructures can also be used for specific enterprise solutions.

5.3.15 *SAP - Digital Cloud Platform*

SAP offers in Leonardo a set of software solutions and microservices that enables customers to leverage innovative technologies such as IoT, machine learning, blockchain, analytics and big data. SAP Leonardo IoT enhances the SAP Cloud Platform, which includes a comprehensive array of industrial protocols, by adding integrated applications and solutions (Miller and Pelino 2018, p. 12). SAP Leonardo is a systematic approach to digitally transforming businesses, focusing on repeatable results across industries. SAP Leonardo accelerates and de-risks digital transformation using methodologies and integrated software components. It brings together design services, a cloud platform and applications, expertise in business processes and technologies such as analytics, Big Data, blockchain, data intelligence, machine learning and IoT (Anon. n.d., p. 10).

With HANA, which is based on the SAP-specific database, SAP follows the philosophy of providing one singular platform and of not offering many disparate products. AI capabilities are integrated via cloud services. The platform is a single digital enterprise foundation, which is open standard-based and based on in-memory technology that scales the expectations of real-time data and enterprise computing in a single platform. The platform is open and cloud-based and offers a comprehensive, cloud-based analytics portfolio that delivers business intelligence, planning, performance management and predictive insight as components of a platform-as-a-service. The HANA platform includes data management, data integration and application development and a front office analytics tool, experience services, design and development applications and management applications which include security features.

The SAP Cloud Platform provides the environment for cloud applications which extend SAP S/4HANA. The cloud integrates business processes, turns real-time data into actions and increases productivity in order that enterprises can make data-driven decisions with predictive analytics and improve automation, efficiency and agility through machine learning.

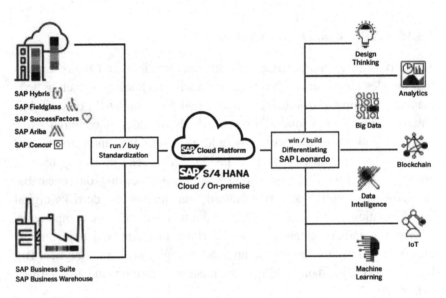

Fig. 5.19. SAP Integrated Cloud Platform System (SAP 2018b, p. 88).

The SAP S/4HANA Cloud is delivered through a software-as-a-service (SaaS) model as a public or private cloud. The platform contains an intelligent core to run business processes in real-time based on a single source of truth, turning large amounts of data into instant, actionable insights and supporting digital transformation through capabilities such as machine learning, scalability and extensibility. It is possible to integrate the SAP S/4HANA Cloud with SAP and third party applications, to extend and configure SAP S/4HANA Cloud processes to suit special needs and to build custom extensions and apps with SAP S/4HANA Cloud SDK and SAP Cloud Platform (SAP 2018c).

The Cloud Platform accelerates app development, mobile apps and customer digital experiences, business transformation processes, extensions and connections with APIs, embedded advanced analytics, innovative Big Data, IoT and machine learning solutions. The data management includes on-premise, hybrid and multi-cloud deployment, in-memory transactions and analytics, data discovery and governance, data orchestration and integration, data cleansing and enrichment and data storage and computing. The enterprise information management includes master data management, data quality and integration, content management, metadata management enterprise architecture and cybersecurity (SAP 2018b).

5.3.16 *Software AG - Cumulocity*

The SoftwareAG offers in Cumulocity an enterprise integration platform-as-a-service (eiPaaS), or a cloud service that addresses IIoT integration and API management capabilities including a variety of scenarios, applications, data integration plans, processes and AI-enabled systems. The IIoT-platform comes with prepackaged solutions that enable the rapid deployment of connected products and services, remote asset condition monitoring and predictive maintenance services

The platform allows enterprises to connect with and manage devices and assets rapidly via SaaS, PaaS and on-premises deployment by use of preconfigured integration solutions. IIoT devices can be controlled remotely, connecting devices and assets over any network, monitoring conditions and generating real-time analytics and reacting immediately to conditions or situations.

Cumulocity IoT offers broad and deep device management capabilities with typical features such as device maintenance and remote diagnostics and provides deployment-scale management of assets through hierarchical multi-level and dynamic rule-based groups. It facilitates mass execution of device lifecycle tasks and device commands.

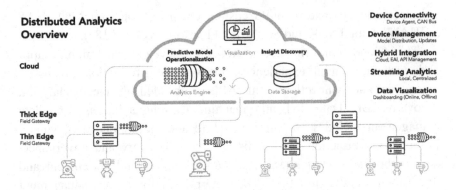

Fig. 5.20. SoftwareAG Predictive Maintenance (SoftwareAG 2018b).

Connectivity management is provided on-platform in the form of device- and aggregate-level data monitoring and device status views and notification and alerting. A device simulator is provided on-platform and uses status data coming directly from sensors and actuators embedded in the equipment (Fig. 5.20). It allows the continuous analysis of data by streaming analytics coupled with predictive models to enable predictive maintenance (SoftwareAG 2018b).

5.4 Conclusion

Digital enterprise integration is not simply connecting applications and databases. In making an integration decision, enterprises have to consider integration technology, the empowerment of integration developers and agility. Digital enterprise integration encompasses traditional and new sophisticated architectures, a wide range of APIs and endpoints, and also new development lifecycles and deployment options. For the enterprise digitalization strategy, it is important to think about integration technology with a focus on integration across hybrid environments rather than focusing on on-premises or cloud data sources only.

Some platform vendors offer comprehensive integration platforms with powerful applications for manufacturing and logistics. Other vendors offer powerful and open IIoT Platforms, which can be used by others to build applications for specific use-cases. Digital enterprise platforms integrate IIoT platforms and edge services designed to extend and evolve with digital enterprise vision. A state-of-the-art IIoT architecture includes device connectivity, messaging, integration, streaming analytics, process modeling, IT portfolio management, machine learning and predictive analytics. When choosing a platform, customers have the choice of platforms with prepackaged software-as-a-service applications as well as platform-as-a service or on-premises solutions.

Connecting a large number of IIoT devices in the enterprise is an absolutely mandatory requirement and enterprises have to be able to connect to nearly anything quickly, whether or not the enterprise has the technical expertise yet. Therefore, teams with a broader set of integration developers are needed to control all aspects of the integration. Enterprises have to scale and adapt fast to required changes. Agility is needed to quickly fulfill the required changes due to the demands of the market, technology changes or customer requirements. Enterprises need to be prepared for major technology waves and each new wave of technological advances requires enterprises to have the ability to incorporate changes quickly and the agility to change and scale quickly. Flexibility is needed for enterprises to be future-ready. Open platforms are an alternative to being ready for future technologies and new trends.

Due to the huge range of software functionality and the rapid changes in the market, a general comparison of the various solutions on the market is difficult, and due to the specific demands of digital enterprises, not even really meaningful. The selection of a system has to be performed individually due to the specific requirements of the particular use-case. Some software vendors, such as Siemens and GE, have a very strong background in automation, others, such as Autodesk, focus more on small and medium businesses, and other vendors, such as AWS, Cisco and Microsoft, offer comprehensive IIoT platforms which can be used with applications from other vendors to build specific solutions.

Chapter 6

Consideration and Future Trends

"It's time to go digital. The digital economy is here and the resulting shift to meet this new reality is accelerating in every industry and compelling every established organization to transform itself into a "Digital Enterprise." All with the goal to not only survive, but thrive in this new social and digital business reality" (Lucas 2016b).

Industrial environments are changing to become digital enterprises and software systems are becoming self-managing, self-tuning and self-healing (Agarwal 2018, p. 11). When getting started with the transformation process into digital enterprises, there is the need to understand the impact and value of digital. It is important to focus not on one area but to consider the interrelationship between all aspects. Further, there is the need to prioritize in the digital portfolio and to focus on important issues because there are always too many things to do. To be successful requires an enterprise to take an end-to-end view, ensuring that customers receive a joined-up experience from end to end and that all functions work well together (Willmott 2013).

Cloud computing and other technologies are opening up new possibilities. Artificial Intelligence especially has increased significantly and machine learning and its subset deep learning continue to advance rapidly, while traditional AI algorithms become more versatile and powerful (Manyika *et al.* 2017, p. 27). During the years between 2016 and 2018 the IIoT has moved very quickly. A Forrester Study (Miller and Pelino 2018) shows that the IIoT is growing big and that potential use cases span from manufacturing and healthcare to consumers. IIoT software platforms are increasingly mature, user interfaces are getting relatively intuitive and the public cloud seems to be the place to be.

Analytics are increasingly a core component of platform solutions. Machine learning and the use of Artificial Intelligence are more common and allow industrial enterprises to move the workings of the enterprise from simply monitoring towards predictive maintenance, machine learning, advanced workload optimization and scheduling. There is a growing interest in connecting IIoT software platforms and application-related enterprise systems. Digital Twins have arrived and augmented reality is on the way (Miller and Pelino 2018, p. 3).

The digital thread makes unprecedented product and process variants attainable and enables traceability across the complete lifecycle, accelerating the development timeline while simultaneously reducing costs. The rise of IIoT platforms lays the foundation to make Digital Twins a reality. Digital Twins offer strong potential to help enterprises achieve better insights into objects and drive better decisions. Nowadays, with increasing computational power and the storage possibilities of big data, the improvement of analytic technologies and the integration of various data enable Digital Twins to model much richer, less isolated and much more sophisticated and realistic models than ever before (Parrott and Warshaw 2017). However, the possibility of adding unnecessary complexity such as a technology overkill for a particular business problem and concerns about cost, security, privacy and integration have to be considered (Shetty 2017).

The disruptive nature of digitalization opens up new business opportunities and ways to satisfy customer requirements more efficiently. Successful transformation requires an end-to-end digital innovation strategy to create comprehensive and precise digital models of products, and production operations to manage the complexity of smart products and smart production operations. Digital Twins provide detailed insight into all aspects of decision-making for product development and production operations, gaining insights from products and plants in operation through use of the IIoT performance (Siemens 2018d). With the cloud as platform and APIs as building blocks for intelligent applications, Artificial Intelligence is available for more people and organizations than ever and the use of unstructured data gives enterprises a competitive advantage.

6.1   Impact on Business Models and Customer Relationship

Digitalization has a significant impact on business models and customer relationships. Digitalization will lead enterprises to move from linear, sequential business operations towards interconnected, open systems, which will change industries and open new ways of realizing and monetizing value. Initiatives might include spawning new business models and developing better, more holistic ways of conducting risk assessments. Digitalization enables enterprises to optimize existing operations and processes and allows them to create strategies and execution plans to deliver deep, contextual experiences, to digitize products, services and processes and also to augment these steps with predictive analytics and cognitive computing, along with IIoT and automation, to create fully integrated, flexible and agile operating environments.

Things are changing. IDC Business Consulting Services predicts (Fig. 6.1) that the potential of cybersecurity and physical safety concerns associated with IIoT devices will pressure enterprises to increase IIoT security. Blockchain-distributed ledgers will incorporate IIoT sensors and Digital Twins will use data from IIoT connected products and assets. Services will be used to implement IIoT solutions and comprehensive analytics capabilities will create outcome-focused functionality. Edge infrastructure will be an important part of IIoT infrastructure and the fifth-generation of wireless will improve connectivity (Turner and MacGillivray 2017).

Digitalization allows enterprises to establish new ways of working, innovation-driven cultures incorporating design thinking, open experimentation and agile working. There is a need to contextualize organizational priorities within business ecosystems, seeking new forms of partnering and new ways to build value within overall systems of engagement.

Moving towards digital enterprises, it has to be considered how enterprises can implement digital strategies ambitious enough to deal with disruption, in order to become more agile, in order to become better equipped to respond immediately to unexpected challenges and opportunities. The automation technologies to be used have to be considered and the workforce has to be open and flexible enough to quickly embrace new ways of working and new strategic priorities (Butner *et al.* 2017, p. 13).

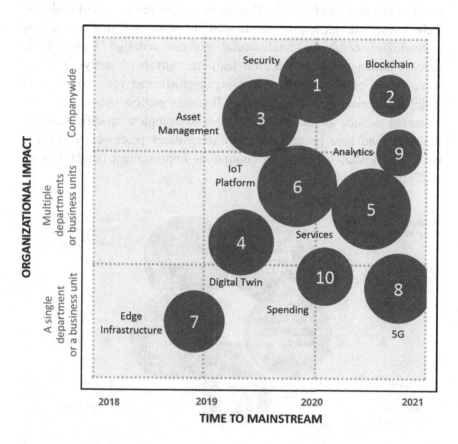

Fig. 6.1. Worldwide IIoT Predictions (Turner and MacGillivray 2017, p. 3).

Holistic decision-making creates the foundation for how enterprises will operate, collaborate and compete in future. The process used for supply handling in production will change from linear supply chains to digital supply networks. Transparency of information across all areas of the supply network and across all functions can improve decision making. The holistic thinking leads to broader strategic transformations. Instead of planning incremental improvements within a supply chain, enterprises can consider how a supply network can be used to fuel growth across the business (Mussomeli *et al*. 2016, p. 8).

To improve the next-generation operating model, there are typically five key capabilities (Fig. 6.2). Digitization improves the use of tools and technology. Intelligent process automation as an emerging set of new technologies combines fundamental process redesign with robotic process automation and machine learning. Advanced analytics is the autonomous processing of data using sophisticated tools to discover insights and make recommendations. Business process outsourcing uses resources outside of the main business to complete specific tasks or functions and lean process redesign streamlines processes, eliminates waste and fosters a culture of continuous improvement (Bollard *et al*. 2017, p. 3).

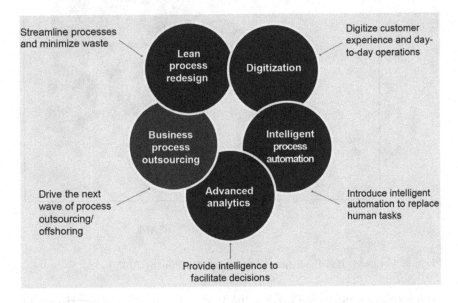

Fig. 6.2. Capabilities of the Next-Generation Operating Model (Bollard *et al*. 2017, p. 4).

New business models and customer relationships will take place. Customers can interact with 3D models of products in virtual reality showrooms and data from each customer interaction can be fed back to product design, research and manufacturing. Similarly, augmented reality mobile apps will replace catalogs and 3D printing will revolutionize rapid prototyping in manufacturing and become more cognitive. These new technologies create engaging experiences for customers, create rich new sources of data and expose new ways gaining value (IBM 2017b, p. 20).

Further digitalization will lead to a paradigm shift in the ways that organizations balance stability and dynamics while moving towards more agile approaches. Due to the strong demand for more flexibility enterprises become more agile. New organizational forms are emerging that balance stability and dynamism and thrive in an era of unprecedented opportunities (Aghina *et al.* 2017, p. 17). Agile organizations require a shared purpose and vision on a strategic level when it comes to sensing and seizing opportunities, flexible resource allocation and actionable strategic guidance. On the structure level these organizations have a clear, flat structure and clear accountable roles in an open physical and virtual environment. On the process level there has to be rapid iteration and experimentation. This should be the standardized way of working. Performance orientation using information transparency and continuous learning enables action-oriented decision-making (Aghina *et al.* 2017, p. 7).

Merging the virtual and the physical worlds through real-time connection, intelligent cyber-physical systems will bring a radical change in the way that factories work to deliver the next evolution of smarter and connected manufacturing. The next generation of smart factory products, resources and processes will automatically re-route work, avoiding bottlenecks and identifying areas of underused capacity. Production customizing and predictive maintenance enables enterprises to operate continuously and at unprecedented levels of efficiency. The smart factory is characterized by cyber-physical systems providing significant real-time quality and advantages in comparison with classic production systems. Manufacturing equipment will be connected and will be able to communicate with other pieces of manufacturing equipment. Sharing real-time information ensures that each participant or device can access all necessary data to be prepared for what is coming next. Information from outside will be accessible, enabling remote control of manufacturing units and services. Machine controllers will be able to access user profiles and maintenance can be carried out more effectively by machine suppliers for manufacturers (Atos 2016, p. 10).

The smart factory as a flexible network of cyber-physical system-based production systems is designed according to sustainable and service-oriented business practices. Flexible production systems include adaptability, self-learning characteristics, fault tolerance and risk management. A smart factory can also be optimized according to a global network of adaptive and self-organizing production units. Smart factory production offers numerous advantages including resource efficient production, optimized production processes determining and identifying fields of activity, configuration options, production conditions and the ability to communicate independently with other units. Smart factories with interfaces to smart mobility, smart logistics and smart grids concepts are an integral component of tomorrow's intelligent infrastructures (Sharma 2018, p. 4).

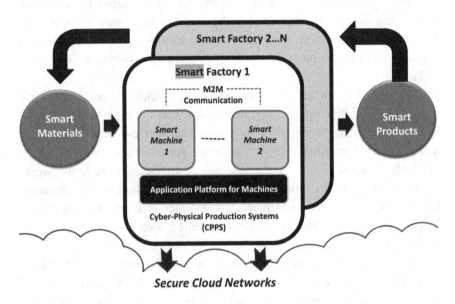

Fig. 6.3. Smart Factory Cloud based Secure Networks (Sharma 2018, p. 5).

Agility is a key requirement for modern enterprise architectures. Agile organizations focus on rapid iteration and experimentation and leverage standardized ways of working to facilitate interaction and communication between teams. These ways of working include the use of digital technologies, and social-networking and advanced meeting formats for teams working together. Agile organizations are performance-oriented by nature and make continuous learning an ongoing, constant part of the processes. Working in rapid cycles requires that agile organizations insist on full transparency of information, so that every team can quickly and easily access the information required and share information with others. Agile organizations emphasize quick, efficient and continuous decision-making, preferring 70 percent probability now to 100 percent certainty later (Aghina *et al.* 2017, p. 14).

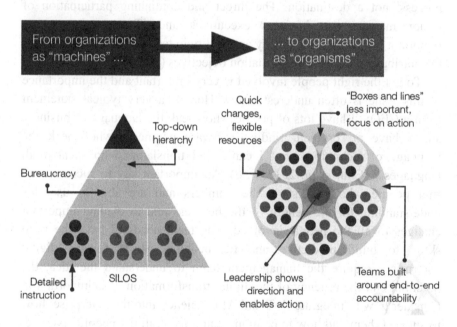

Fig. 6.4. Agile Organizations are Living Organisms (Aghina *et al.* 2017, p. 5).

Agile enterprises have a good chance of being in the top quartile of organizational health and simultaneously achieving greater customer centricity, faster time-to-market, higher revenue growth, lower costs and a more engaged workforce (Aghina *et al.* 2017, p. 17).

6.2 Changes in Management, Leadership and Organization

The impact of digitalization is not related to technical issues only. There is also a significant impact on management, leadership and organizational issues. When implementing digital enterprises in industrial praxis it is important to consider that available data are growing exponentially and advanced analytics offers new possibilities. With more data from a huge number of devices learning can be improved, but many organizations are struggling to turn data into value (Chin *et al.* 2017, p. 2). A key factor for success is to manage the digital transformation. A digital transformation has to support enterprise business objectives at a high level and is a process, not a destination. The direct and continuing participation of senior management, business executives and IT management are important for success. Flexibility and agility in technology investment has to contribute to digital transformation objectives (IDC 2017, p. 16).

To get the right people involved is very important and the importance of this issue is often underestimated. Here is a very typical statement from a CEO: "I have lots of people who speak the language of business and I have no problem finding software engineers who speak the language of technology, but I can't find translators who speak both languages." (Chin *et al.* 2017, p. 6). An important key to success is to find people who understand the numbers and are able to use this understanding for the benefit of the business and to explain important changes to all the people involved. The team needs to have the right skills to build predictive analytic insights. Shifts toward digital enterprises require the management team to understand the idea, the potential and the urgency of the digital transformation. It is important to consider how to integrate IIoT and AI efficiency into the enterprise, how to support them and how to communicate this to all the people involved. Further it has to be considered that change is often stressful. Managing employee stress and well-being is going to be an important aspect of changing future work (Atos 2018d, p. 10).

6.3 Impact on Jobs, Education, Training and Learning

Advances in robotics, Artificial Intelligence and machine learning are leading to a new age of automation. Machines match or outperform humans in a range of work activities, including ones requiring cognitive capabilities. Technical, economic and social factors will determine the pace and extent of automation. Individuals in the workplace will need to engage more comprehensively with machines as part of their daily activities and acquire new skills due to the rising demand for these skills in a new automation age. This will include rethinking education and training, income support and safety nets, and also transition support for those who have been dislocated (Manyika *et al.* 2017, p. 3).

Automation is not a new phenomenon and questions regarding its impact on employment and on productivity in the global economy are also not new. The fear of technological innovation destroying jobs and displacing workers dates back several hundred years. A McKinsey Study (Manyika *et al.* 2017) estimates that people displaced by automation will find other employment. A look at history teaches us about the effect of technological changes on work, employment and productivity, and that the deployment of new technologies in the past has always led to new forms of work. Some jobs disappeared and new ones were created, although what those new jobs would be could not be predicted at the time. The question today is whether this latest wave of innovation is by its nature substantially different from technological disruptions in the past (Manyika *et al.* 2017, pp. 31-32).

Robotics, AI, sensors and cognitive computing have gone mainstream. As robotics and AI are integrated, the emphasis on workforce skills in the enterprise is shifting significantly towards complex problem-solving skills, cognitive abilities, process and resource management and social skills. Physical abilities will be less important (Agarwal *et al.* 2018, p. 75). Leading organizations are rethinking work architecture, retraining people and rearranging the organization to leverage technology to transform business. The broader aim is not just to eliminate routine tasks and cut costs, but to create value for customers and meaningful work for people (Agarwal *et al.* 2018, p. 77).

Artificial Intelligence is converting the unstructured work patterns of the past into the advanced workflows of the future (IBM 2017b, p. 8). But even with the increasing intelligence of machines, people will remain important. Human-centric plant strategies will enable a flexible and proactive production environment and humans will retain the fundamental control and decision-making functions. Intelligent, self-aware machines will liberate operators to focus on optimizing production and planning. Cross-functional communications will be enabled along the entire value chain, from design through engineering, production, sales and service. Industrial Internet and mobility will converge in any device at any time and any place. The tablet that did not exist some years ago has already become the device of choice for a whole generation. Permanent access to live information feeds and automatic alerts from the machines to mobile devices, will allow operators, managers and engineers to move around more safely in the knowledge that the access to the latest status information is always available anywhere. Decision-making and actions can be performed from any location (Atos 2016, p. 10).

The future of manufacturing in Digital Enterprises is still people-centric, even if some roles may disappear or fundamentally change. But skills and knowledge will intensify in importance. Automation and rapid production require workers with faster decision-making abilities to become and remain experts. In this context, supporting new workforce scenarios and realigning roles will be more fundamental than ever. Considerable organizational and cultural work will be needed to engage and motivate traditional workers by aligning traditional expertise with the needs of the changing production environment and to attract younger employees used to a more open collaborative way of working (Atos 2016, p. 10).

Therefore, for humans the nature of job roles and the style of work, education and learning will change tremendously. The future of work has been transformed by automation and therefore requires a reskilling of the workforce. Low-skill tasks are increasingly automated and more sophisticated equipment requires skilled operators with new capabilities to run these systems. Managers and supervisors are increasingly supported by powerful software tools and will spend less time on tracking daily performance. This gives them more time to manage teams and to look for innovative opportunities on a strategic level.

The new focus is on a flexible workforce and on social skills. Training opportunities regarding soft skills are increasingly important. Because change is stressful, the management has to deal with employee stress and social well-being (Atos 2018d). New roles such as change agents are increasingly important. Change agents have the difficult job of identifying issues, developing and implementing solutions, building capabilities and changing mind-sets. Due to the changes required by the digital transformation process, the capabilities to guide colleagues through significant changes will become increasingly important.

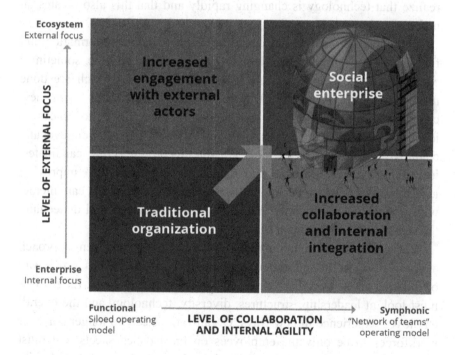

Fig. 6.5. Evolution towards the Social Enterprise (Agarwal *et al.* 2018, p. 3).

As they move towards digitalization, enterprises require a shift from traditional organizational structures towards social enterprises (Fig. 6.5). In social enterprises, it is required to listen very carefully to all parties involved in the internal and external environment. It is important to take advantage of the available data. The increasingly connected nature of the workplace means that interactions between and among workers and the outside world can be a tremendous source for analysis if managed appropriately (Agarwal *et al.* 2018, p. 3).

Technological changes have unforeseen impacts on society. New communication technologies and advances in Artificial Intelligence are fundamentally changing how work is performed and how it influences society. Machine learning was not in the mainstream a few years ago and now it is simultaneously one of the hottest disruption areas and a source of tremendous anxiety about potential job losses. People increasingly realize that technology is changing rapidly and that this also creates an unforeseen impact on social cohesion (Agarwal *et al.* 2018, p. 4).

Embedded AI can predict what people need, deliver information and functionality via the right medium at the right place and time, sometimes even before people need it, and automate many tasks which are done manually today (Agarwal 2018, p. 5). AI and robotics open new capabilities for HR. Software can recognize faces, listen to voices or identify mood and decode video interviews to identify education level and cognitive ability. Analytics tools are intelligently selecting candidates, identifying career options and coaching managers on improving leadership skills. AI is even being used to create chatbots that can interact with job candidates, identify and score video interviews and understand the sentiment of engagement surveys.

These trends require adopting a human capital management approach and will result in the redesign of almost every job, as well as a new way of thinking about workforce planning and the nature of work. Enterprises must look at leadership, structures, diversity, technology and the overall employee experience in new ways. Organizations can no longer consider workforces to be only the employees on the balance sheets, but must include freelancers and others. Workers have to be augmented with machines and software (Deloitte 2018b, p. 14).

For successful digital reinvention, enterprises need to pursue a new strategic focus, build new expertise and establish new ways of working (Butner *et al.* 2017, p. 8). Industrial businesses in digital enterprises have the opportunity to develop new ways of realizing and monetizing value, spawning new business models and using new forms of processes and more holistic ways of conducting risk assessments (Fig. 6.6). New expertise is required to digitize products, services and processes and to augment these steps with predictive analytics and cognitive computing, along with IIoT and automation, to create fully integrated, flexible and agile operating environments. New ways of working have to be established, and industrial businesses will need to identify and build digital organizations incorporating design thinking, agile working, open experimentation and value-building within overall systems of engagement enabled by digital capabilities (Butner *et al.* 2017, p. 9).

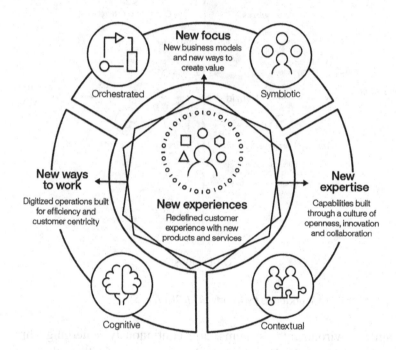

Fig. 6.6. Digital Reinvention Operating Environment (Butner *et al.* 2017, p. 8).

Further, the type of workforce is changing from one employing traditional workers to one employing outside contractors, tenured remote workers and transactional remote workers (Fig. 6.7). The way that work is done varies from short-term relationships with transactional remote workers to longer-term relationships accelerating learning and performance improvement. Work becomes more creative and will be carried out by small teams or work groups that will collaborate on different projects over extended periods of time (Schwartz *et al.* 2017, p. 4).

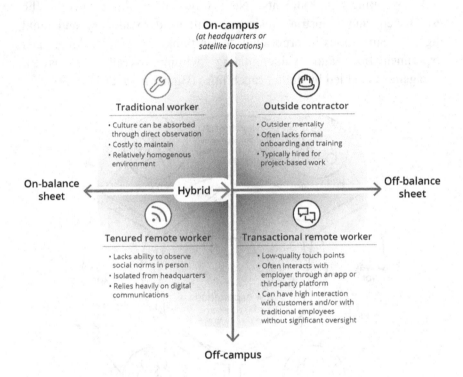

Fig. 6.7. Alternative Workforces (Schwartz *et al.* 2017, p. 5).

In agile environments, systems are continuously emerging through experimentation and adaptation. Agile performance cells include cross-functional teams defining a vision and prioritizing work across products and projects. Self-managing teams define the best way to reach goals, prioritize activities and focus on effort. Work pools of individuals enhance efficiency, enabling people to build broader skillsets and ensure that business priorities are adequately resourced (Aghina *et al.* 2017, p. 11).

Education, training and learning are changing significantly with digitalization. It has to be considered that technology and the type of workforce will continuously change and everybody involved has to keep on learning during all phases of their lifetime. Therefore adult learning gets more important. Emphasis is placed on designing programs and combining methods like on-the-job training, in-person-learning and online refresher courses (Chin *et al.* 2017, p. 6). Due to rapid technology changes the half-life period of knowledge is decreasing significantly and the knowledge of facts is increasingly less important. Specific facts can be found very quickly for each area by use of the Internet or the Intranet of an enterprise. Nowadays, the much more important qualification is the ability to find the specific information and to differentiate important and reliable information from not so important or unreliable information.

Modern education has to focus on a good understanding of fundamentals, such as mathematical, mechanical, electrical, computer, business and other fundamentals. The further abilities of system analysis and project management are also relevant. Social skills and the ability of lifelong learning are much more important than specific technical facts. Based on this modern education, advanced training on the job provided by the use of modern communication technologies will change classical education structures tremendously.

6.4 Change Management towards Digital Twins

When moving towards digital enterprises, a strong change management initiative is required to manage the expected changes and to calculate the effort that has to be made by organizations and leadership. The change management initiative has to consider questions about how much business input is sufficient and the expected value to be harvested from the proposed solutions. Also important are how fast changes can be made and how to inspire all the people involved in the change.

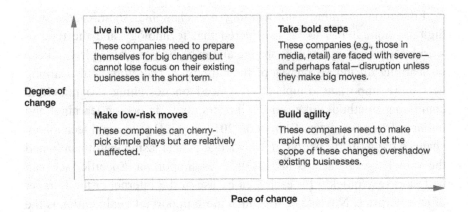

Fig. 6.8. Response on Disruptions (Bughin *et al.* 2018, p. 13).

Since the extent and speed of disruptions varies, enterprises will need to find the best response (Fig. 6.8). Changing systems always raises the question if changes should be performed in large steps as a system revolution or in many small steps as a system evolution. Independent of the selected approach, optimizing never ends and there is still a need for the continuous improvement of enterprise systems. To enable changes, the speed and efficiency of the changes and optimization process is important. In industrial praxis it is normally not required to find an absolute (100%) optimum. It is better to have a good solution which is available fast. On the operational level, the requirement is to find a good solution in nearly real-time and not to look for the best solution available after a long time (Bughin *et al.* 2018, p. 13).

The curriculum of change should include not only technology and data but also the leadership skills required to lead the identification and implementation of a use case end-to-end and to lead culture change. People buy into changes when they understand the idea and feel that they are integrated as an active part of the change process. The design of solutions therefore needs to be user-led and to include participation from the beginning. The change management initiative requires people who understand technology and can also apply it to the business and lead use-case development from start to finish (Chin *et al.* 2017, p. 4).

Starting digital enterprise projects requires one to have a clear idea of the benefits of digital technologies including the potential impact on the particular business. It is essential to think big, to develop a vision and clear strategy for future developments and then to begin with a small step. Change management has to guide the transition towards digital enterprises. With smaller stakes, strategies can be tested and refined with relatively minor consequences. Selecting projects at the edges of the enterprise can provide greater latitude for building digital capabilities and can also help individuals to feel less afraid to fail, which ultimately leads to greater innovation. It is advisable not to wait for perfect solutions, but to start with single prioritized transformations which could potentially lead to gains in value. At the same time, it is essential to act with growth in mind and to focus on areas that might unlock several waves of potential value, creating a ripple effect that leads to exponential growth.

By starting small and moving quickly, enterprises can generate success that proves the value and importance of digitalization. Success generates success, as sharing examples of successful digitalization can convince skeptics within the enterprise and also demonstrate to customers that the enterprise is focusing on improvement. Advancing to digital enterprises is not about a single technology implementation, it is more about developing an agile culture using expert resources as part of the network and promoting a strategic approach towards advancing business strategies.

As we shift towards digital enterprises, some key questions have to be answered: What can an enterprise do to make digital strategies ambitious enough to deal with disruption? How can enterprises become more agile in order to be better equipped to respond to unexpected challenges and opportunities? How can workforces be made open and flexible enough to quickly embrace new ways of working and new strategic priorities? What actions can help enterprises to let leadership be more visionary in conceiving what customers want before they know it themselves? How can IIoT, robotics and automation technologies differentiate and achieve advanced operational efficiencies (Butner *et al.* 2017, p. 15)?

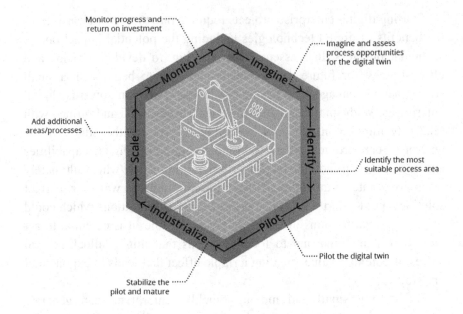

Fig. 6.9. Getting Started with the Digital Twin (Parrott and Warshaw 2017, p. 13).

When getting started with Digital Twins (Fig. 6.9), the first step is to imagine the possibilities that could arise from having a Digital Twin. The second step is to identify a process for a pilot application with the highest possible value and the best chance of being successful. Moving into a pilot program, iterative and agile cycles can be applied to accelerate learning, manage risk proactively and maximize return on investments. Once the pilot is successfully running, the Digital Twin development and deployment process can be industrialized and opportunities to scale the Digital Twin can be identified. Changes to the processes have to be performed iteratively in order to identify the best possible configuration. The value realized through the Digital Twin has to be measured and when starting a new cycle, the possibilities for the next applications of Digital Twins in the enterprise have to be imagined (Parrott and Warshaw 2017, p. 13).

Digital Twins have the strong potential to achieve better insights into objects and to drive better decisions. However, realizing Digital Twins requires some understanding. When using Digital Twins to enable disruptive IIoT solutions and business outcomes, one should focus on objectives, understanding the key business benefits before investing in Digital Twins. In general, simplicity should be the first priority. Models should be as simple as possible and as complex as required. Even if Digital Twins offer a very powerful advantage, the building of complex Digital Twins should be avoided if business objectives can meet the goal with basic indicators. In the long-term, new business models will emerge, facilitated by Digital Twins, such as the selling of physical object-related performance data or the practice of charging for objects based on performance data (Shetty 2017, p. 3).

In future, Digital Twin applications will increasingly move towards AI decision-making. For AI algorithms the data are one key to success and it is crucial to determine the type, quantity and quality of data. By starting small, it is possible to release an application faster and then build on it over time. It is crucial to accept failure as an integral part of innovation that contributes to organizational learning. AI applications can be iteratively extended to scale and Digital Twins can expand their capabilities and capture increasing value over time.

6.5 Strategic Future Trends

In the fields of technology and communication, there has been a shift towards digitalization. Some years ago, nobody would have estimated how much is possible with modern information technology such as mobiles today. There is already a tremendous change, and rich data, connectivity with real-time communication and Artificial Intelligence will change the way companies work and communicate (Gupta and Ulrich 2017).

The Industrial Internet of Things (IIoT) and digitalization are already reality, offering opportunities for product and business model innovation which could not have been imagined a few years ago. Seamless integration of data from a large number of intelligent devices is feeding software solutions like design and simulation software. Digital services tailored to specific use cases will allow unmatched transparency and opportunities along the entire value chain. IIoT with scalable connectivity and easy-to-use tools for application building and commercialization offer vast opportunities to leverage domain-specific know-how for building digital revenue streams. A critical success factor for the future of business is the ability to close the loop to realize the Digital Twin and to leverage domain-specific solutions and services, thus turning data into value.

An exact estimation of how the future will develop is not possible. However, in the following sections some likely strategic technology trends for future development shall be discussed. Research on future technology trends has been performed for some years by the Gartner company, and their vision of strategic technology trends is published once a year. Most of these trends are focusing on digital environments using advanced strategies and Artificial Intelligence. The top strategic technology trends for the year 2019 (Panetta 2018), 2018 (Panetta 2017) and 2017 (Panetta 2016) can be summarized as:

Trend: Artificial Intelligence Foundation and Development

The ability to use Artificial Intelligence to enhance decision making and reinvent business models and ecosystems. Machine learning and advanced Artificial Intelligence will be the most significant future trend; it offers capabilities and achieves possibilities that even a couple of years ago seemed to be impossible. AI-driven development looks at tools, technologies and best practices for embedding AI into applications and using AI to create AI-powered tools for the development process.

Trend: Intelligent Applications and Augmented Analytics

Over the next few years every application, software and service will incorporate Artificial Intelligence at some level. AI will run in the background of many application categories and intelligent apps will create a new intelligent intermediary layer between people and systems. Augmented analytics is a particularly strategic growing area that uses machine learning to automate data preparation, insight discovery and insight sharing for a broad range of business users, operational workers and data scientists.

Trend: Intelligent and Autonomous Things

Intelligent things use machine learning and Artificial Intelligence to interact in a more intelligent way with people and their surroundings. These things operate semi-autonomously or autonomously in an unsupervised environment for a set amount of time to complete a particular task. As the technology develops, machine learning and AI will increasingly appear in a variety of objects ranging from smart equipment to autonomous robots. As intelligent things proliferate, a shift from stand-alone intelligent things to a swarm of collaborative intelligent things offers new and enhanced possibilities. The sophistication of the intelligence varies, but all autonomous things use AI to interact more naturally with their environments.

Trend: Digital Twins

Digital Twins are digital representations of real-world entities or systems. As the physical object is changing, the data from it is being collected and replicated in a virtual digital equivalent. In the context of IIoT, Digital Twins are linked to real-world objects and offer information on the state of their counterparts, respond to changes, improve operations and add value. Digital Twins will offer help with asset management, operational efficiency, maintenance repair and insights into how products are used and how they can be improved. With AI-based capabilities, Digital Twins will enable advanced simulation, operation and analysis.

Trend: Empowered Edge Computing

Edge computing is a computing topology in which information processing, content collection and delivery are placed closer to the sources of information to keep traffic local and to reduce latency. Connectivity and latency challenges, bandwidth constraints and greater functionality embedded at the edge favors distributed models. Enterprises should begin using edge design patterns in the infrastructure architectures, particularly for those with significant IIoT elements. This type of architecture will allow a different level of flexibility and a faster development pace.

Trend: Conversational Platforms

Conversational platforms will drive a paradigm shift in which the burden of translating intent shifts from user to computer and systems are capable of simple answers or more complicated interactions. These platforms will continue to evolve to become capable of even more complex actions, such as collecting oral testimony and acting on that information to deliver complex outcomes.

Trend: Augmented and Virtual Reality

Augmented Reality (AR), Virtual Reality (VR) and Mixed Reality are changing the way that people perceive and interact with the digital world. Combined with conversational platforms, a fundamental shift in the user experience will emerge. Experiences will become more invisible and more immersive. Over the next five years the focus will be on mixed reality, which is emerging as the immersive experience of choice, where the user interacts with digital and real-world objects while maintaining a presence in the physical world.

Trend: Blockchain

Blockchain is a shared, distributed, decentralized and tokenized ledger that removes business friction by being independent of individual applications or participants. Blockchain adds trust, in an automated sense, and allows various parties to perform commercial and technical transactions.

Trend: Event-Driven

Digital businesses rely on the ability to sense and to be ready to exploit new digital business moments. Business events reflect the discovery of notable states or state changes, such as the completion of a purchase order. Some events or combinations of events constitute a situation that calls for a specific action to be performed. With the advent of AI, the IIoT and other technologies, events can be detected more quickly and analyzed in greater detail.

Trend: Smart Spaces

Smart spaces are physical or digital environments in which humans and technology-enabled systems interact in increasingly open, connected, coordinated and intelligent ecosystems. Smart devices will deliver increasingly insightful digital services everywhere and AI-driven technology, edge computing, blockchain and Digital Twins are contributing to this trend as individual solutions become smart spaces.

Trend: Continuous Adaptive Risk and Trust

Digital business creates a complex, evolving security environment. Continuous adaptive risk and trust assessment allows for real-time, risk and trust-based decision-making with adaptive responses to security-enabled digital business. The digital world requires embracing people-centric security and empowering developers to take responsibility for security measures.

Trend: Digital Ethics and Privacy

Consumers have a growing awareness of the value of personal information and are increasingly concerned about how data are used by public and private entities. Enterprises that do not pay attention are at risk of consumer backlash.

This research on future technology trends performed by the Gartner company (Panetta 2018; Panetta 2017; Panetta 2016), can give us a vision of the direction in which things may move. However, the details of what really will happen in the economy and in production and logistic enterprises are not really predictable. Where will we be in ten, fifteen or twenty years? To predict what really will happen in the future, we need a crystal ball. In order to get an idea of future trends, it is sometimes meaningful to get some idea of what had been promoted or predicted in the past and how things have worked out in reality later on. Even predictions from IT experts about IT can go wrong. Here are two examples which absolutely didn't come true. One is the estimation from Ken Olsen (CEO, Digital Corp.) in 1977, "There is no reason anyone would want a computer in their home (Schofield 2011)." The other is from Bill Gates (CEO, Microsoft) in 1995, "The internet is just a passing fad (Gates 1995)." From our present vantage point, we know that things have moved quite differently. Most computers are used at home or as mole devices for private use, and the Internet is a key component in modern IT. The Digital Equipment Corporation (DEC), co-founded by Ken Olsen in 1957, had been the world's second-largest computer company, with more than 100,000 employees. But due to their poor estimation of future trends, the company went down and was acquired in 1998 by Compaq (Schofield 2011). Bill Gates revised his statement and Microsoft is nowadays an important player in the Internet.

Even if an exact estimation of how the future of digital enterprises will develop is not possible, one fact is clear. The future will move further on and things will change increasingly quickly. Often these changes are much faster and have much more impact than managers from leading companies have predicted in the past. The speed of changes is increasing and the ability to deal with changes will be increasingly important in all areas of life and business. There has always been some exciting visionary who has turned his vision into a successful business by developing strong innovative visions and making these into realities.

The future is starting now and digitalization is at the heart of enterprises strategies. A successful operation involving digital enterprise systems with Digital Twins and Artificial Intelligence requires one to think big and develop innovative leading strategies for the digital enterprise. To be a disrupter, rather than being disrupted, innovative positions and strategies for the future have to be applied. It helps to focus on priority areas first, to start small but really quickly and then grow, to scale and expand on the base of already successful implementations and to always keep agile and adapt the strategies towards changing future demands. This strategy is not new. Already, Steve Jobs has stated (Device Inside 2018): "Start small, think big, don't worry about too many things at once, take a handful of simple things to begin with, and then progress to more complex ones. Think about not just tomorrow, but the future."

Abbreviations

3D	Three Dimensional
6D	Six Dimensional (3D translative, 3D rotatory)
AAF	Agile Architecture Framework
AGI	Artificial General Intelligence
AI	Artificial Intelligence
ALM	Application Lifecycle Management
AM	Additive Manufacturing
ANI	Artificial Narrow Intelligence
ANN	Artificial Neural Network
API	Application Programming Interfaces
APM	Asset Performance Management
APQP	Advanced Product Quality Planning
APS	Advanced Planning and Scheduling
AR	Augmented Reality
ASI	Artificial Super Intelligence
AWS	Amazon Web Services
BJ	Binder Jetting
BOM	Bill of Materials
C3	Company
CAD	Computer Aided Design
CAE	Computer Aided Engineering
CAM	Computer Aided Manufacturing
CEO	Chief Executive Officer
CLM	Collaborative Lifecycle Management
CLM	Closed Loop Manufacturing
CLQ	Closed Loop Quality
CNC	Computerized Numerical Control
CNN	Convolutional Neural Networks
CPO	Code of PLM Openness
CPS	Cyber-Physical Systems
CRM	Customer Relationship Management

CX	Customer Experience
DA	Design Automation
DDD	Domain Driven Design
DEC	Digital Equipment Corporation
DLP	Digital Light Processing
DMLS	Direct Metal Laser Sintering
DNA	Deoxyribonucleic Acid
DOD	Drop on Demand
DSN	Digital Supply Network
EAM	Enterprise Asset Management
EBM	Electron Beam Melting
ECAD	Electronic Computer Aided Design
EDA	Electronic Design Automation
EMI	Electronic Manufacturing Intelligence
ePLM	Extended Product Lifecycle Management
ERP	Enterprise Resource Planning
FDM	Fused Deposition Modeling
FFF	Fused Filament Fabrication
FFNN	Feed Forward Neural Networks
FMEA	Failure Mode Effects Analysis
GAN	Generative Adversarial Networks
GE	General Electric
IA	Intelligent Automation
IDC	IDC Business Consulting Services
IEC	International Electrotechnical Commission
IEEE	Institute of Electrical and Electronics Engineers
IIoT	Industrial Internet of Things
IoT	Internet of Things
ISO	Industry Standard Organization
IT	Information Technology
JIS	Just-in-Sequence
JIT	Just-in-Time
LA	Lifecycle Analytics
LoRa	Long Range
LPWAN	Low Power Wide Area Networks
MaaS	Manufacturing-as-a-Service
MCAD	Mechanical Computer Aided Design
MES	Manufacturing Execution System
MJ	Material Jetting
ML	Machine Learning
MOM	Manufacturing Operations Management
MTO	Make-to-Order

NASA	National Aeronautics and Space Administration
NC	Numerical Control
OPC	Open Platform Communications
OPC UA	Open Platform Communications Unified Architecture
PaaS	Platform-as-a-Service
PC	Personal Computer
PDM	Product Data Management
PLC	Programmable Logic Controller
PLM	Product Lifecycle Management
QMS	Quality Management System
QoS	Quality of Service
RNN	Recurrent Neural Networks
RPA	Robotic Process Automation
SaaS	Software-as-a-Service
SCADA	Supervisory Control and Data Acquisition
SDK	Software Development Kit
SLA	Stereolithography
SLM	Selective Laser Melting
SLS	Selective Laser Sintering
SOA	Service Oriented Architecture
TIA	Totally Integrated Automation
TQM	Total Quality Management
TSN	Time-Sensitive Networking
UV	Ultra Violet
VPN	Virtual Private Network
VR	Virtual Reality
VRC	Virtual Robot Controller

Bibliography

Adams, M., Kühn, W., Stör, T., and Zelm, M., 2007. IEC 62264. The new standard for interoperability of manufacturing operations and enterprise management. ATP, 49, 52–64.

Agarwal, D., Bersin, J., Lahiri, G., Schwartz, J., and Volini, E., 2018. The Rise of the Social Enterprise [online]. Available from: https://www2.deloitte.com/content/dam/insights/us/articles/HCTrends2018/2018-HCtrends_Rise-of-the-social-enterprise.pdf [Accessed 7 Oct 2018].

Agarwal, S., 2018. 10 Predictions For Software Developers in 2018 [online]. Available from: http://www.oracle.com/technetwork/articles/oracle-dev-2018-predictions-4364393.pdf [Accessed 7 Aug 2018].

Aghina, W., De Smet, A., and Weerda, K., 2015. Agility: It Rhymes With Stability [online]. Available from: https://www.mckinsey.com/business-functions/organization/our-insights/agility-it-rhymes-with-stability#0 [Accessed 7 Aug 2018].

Aghina, W., De Smet, A., Lackey, G., Lurie, M., and Murarka, M., 2017. The Five Trademarks of Agile Organizations [online]. Available from: https://www.mckinsey.com/business-functions/organization/our-insights/the-five-trademarks-of-agile-organizations#0 [Accessed 8 Oct 2018].

Ahlbaeck, K., Fahrbach, C., Murarka, M., and Salo, O., 2017. How to Create an Agile Organization [online]. Available from: https://www.mckinsey.com/business-functions/organization/our-insights/how-to-create-an-agile-organization#0 [Accessed 8 Oct 2018].

AllDP, 2018. 3D Printing Technology Guide [online]. Available from: https://all3dp.com/1/types-of-3d-printers-3d-printing-technology/ [Accessed 20 Dec 2018].

Alsén, D., Patel, P., Shangkuan, J., and Shangkuan, J., 2017. The Future of Connectivity: Enabling the Internet of Things [online]. Available from: https://www.mckinsey.com/global-themes/internet-of-things/our-insights/the-future-of-connectivity-enabling-the-internet-of-things [Accessed 7 Aug 2018].

Amazon Web Services, 2018. AWS Greengrass [online]. Available from: https://aws.amazon.com/greengrass/.

Anon., 2017. Artificial Intelligence Defined (Part 1). Available from: https://www2.deloitte.com/se/sv/pages/technology/articles/part1-artificial-intelligence-defined.html.

Anon., 2018. Amazon Web Services (AWS) - Cloud Computing Services [online]. Available from: https://aws.amazon.com/?nc2=h_lg.

Anon., n.d. SAP Leonardo | Intelligent Technologies [online]. Available from: https://www.sap.com/products/leonardo.html#pdf-asset=e033a960-057d-0010-87a3-c30de2ffd8ff&page=2.

Aras, 2016. Aras Innovator Security: Protecting Your Product Assets [online]. Available from: https://www.aras.com/en/resources/white-papers/aras-innovator-security-white-paper [Accessed 7 Aug 2018].

Aras, 2017. Product Complexity, Digital Transformation, and the Innovation Imperative: The Race to Reinvent How Complex Products Are Developed Is Here [online]. Available from: https://www.aras.com/papers/WHITE-PAPER-aras-plm-product-innovation-platform.pdf [Accessed 7 Aug 2018].

Aras, 2018a. An Overview of Aras Innovator [online]. Available from: https://www.aras.com/plm-software/?n=aras-innovator-overview-plm-software [Accessed 7 Aug 2018].

Aras, 2018b. The Aras PLM Platform [online]. Available from: https://www.aras.com [Accessed 7 Nov 2018].

Atos, 2016. Smart Factory [online]. Available from: https://atos.net/wp-content/uploads/2016/07/atos-smart-factory-ascent-thought-leadership-whitepaper.pdf [Accessed 11 Nov 2018].

Atos, 2018a. Codex AI Suite The Fast-Track to Artificial Intelligence [online]. Available from: https://atos.net/wp-content/uploads/2018/06/Atos-Codex-AI-Suite-Positioning-paper.pdf [Accessed 11 Nov 2018].

Atos, 2018b. Codex Datalake Engine [online]. Available from: https://atos.net/wp-content/uploads/2018/10/Atos-Datalake-Engine.pdf [Accessed 11 Nov 2018].

Atos, 2018c. Google Cloud and Atos Form a Global Partnership to Deliver Secure Hybrid Cloud, Machine Learning and Collaboration Solutions to the Enterprise [online]. Available from: https://atos.net/wp-content/uploads/2018/04/google-Cloud-and-atos-form-a-global-partnership.pdf [Accessed 11 Nov 2018].

Atos, 2018d. Future of Work [online]. Available from: https://atos.net/wp-content/uploads/2018/06/atos-cio-watercooler-transitioning-to-the-future-of-work-cio-views.pdf [Accessed 24 Nov 2018].

Autodesk, 2016. Realize the Future of Making Things with a Product Innovation Platform [online]. Available from: https://synergiscadblog.com/wp-content/uploads/2016/12/product-innovation-platform-whitepaper-en.pdf [Accessed 8 Nov 2018].

Autodesk, 2018a. FUSION 360 [online]. Available from: https://www.autodesk.com/products/fusion-360 [Accessed 7 Aug 2018].

Autodesk, 2018b. FUSION PRODUCTION [online]. Available from: https://www.autodesk.com/products/fusion-production/features [Accessed 12 Oct 2018].

AWS, 2018a. AWS IoT Core [online]. Available from: https://aws.amazon.com/iot-core/.

AWS, 2018b. AWS IoT Analytics Overview [online]. Available from: https://aws.amazon.com/iot-analytics/.

Bailey, J., 2018. Everything You Need to Know About Asset Performance Management [online]. Available from: https://www.ge.com/digital/blog/everything-you-need-know-about-asset-performance-management [Accessed 11 Oct 2018].

Barbazange, H., Beijer, P., Bunouf, J.-M., Kinson, C., Le, F., Le, J.-P., Lonjon, A., and Regnier, J., 2018. Agile Architecture in the Digital Age [online]. Available from: https://publications.opengroup.org/downloadable/download/link/id/MC45MDA3O DUwMCAxNTM5MTYxODE2MjM1NjY2MjQ1MDUyOTU1/ [Accessed 10 Oct 2018].

Behrendt, A., Karunakaran, S., Kelly, R., and Nanry, J., 2017. We Are Living in a Digitally Disrupted World [online]. Available from: https://www.mckinsey.com/business-functions/operations/our-insights/we-are-living-in-a-digitally-disrupted-world [Accessed 8 Aug 2018].

Berruti, F., Chandratre, G., and Rab, Z., 2018. The New Frontier: Agile Automation at Scale [online]. Available from: https://www.mckinsey.com/~/media/McKinsey/Business%20Functions/Operations /Our%20Insights/The%20new%20frontier%20Agile%20automation%20at%20scal e/The-new-frontier-Agile-automation-at-scale.ashx [Accessed 4 Oct 2018].

Boehm, J., Merrath, P., Riemenschnitter, R., Stähle, T., and Poppensieker, T., 2018. Cyber Risk Measurement and the Holistic Cybersecurity Approach [online]. Available from: https://www.mckinsey.com/business-functions/risk/our-insights/cyber-risk-measurement-and-the-holistic-cybersecurity-approach?cid=other-eml-alt-mip-mck-oth-1811&hlkid=c0daad3b6cdf461f9a5fbd5beaf94692&hctky=10322662&hdpid=2d7 1440f-329f-4038-8100-e353a5c2d01f [Accessed 20 Nov 2018].

Bollard, A., Duncan, E., Rangelov, P., and Rohr, M., 2017. Accelerating The Shift to a Next-Generation Operating Model [online]. Available from: https://www.mckinsey.com/~/media/McKinsey/Business%20Functions/McKinsey %20Digital/Our%20Insights/Accelerating%20the%20shift%20to%20a%20next-generation%20operating%20model/Accelerating-the-shift-to-a-next-generation-operating-model.ashx [Accessed 7 Aug 2018].

Bollard, A., Larrea, E., Alex, S., and Sood, R., 2017. The Next-Generation Operating Model for the Digital World [online]. Available from: https://www.mckinsey.com/~/media/McKinsey/Business%20Functions/McKinsey %20Digital/Our%20Insights/The%20next%20generation%20operating%20model %20for%20the%20digital%20world/The-next-generation-operating-model-for-the-digital-world.ashx [Accessed 7 Aug 2018].

Bourne, V., 2018. Vanson Bourne: IoT – The Platform for Success [online]. Available from: https://resources.softwareag.com/iot/vanson-bourne-research-iot-platform-for-success-white-paper.

Buck, C., 2018. A Milestone for Industry [online]. Pictures of the Future. Available from: https://www.siemens.com/innovation/en/home/pictures-of-the-future/industry-and-automation/the-future-of-manufacturing-time-sensitive-networking.html [Accessed 7 Aug 2018].

Bughin, J., Catlin, T., Hirt, M., and Willmott, P., 2018. Why Digital Strategies Fail [online]. Available from: https://www.mckinsey.com/business-functions/digital-mckinsey/our-insights/why-digital-strategies-fail [Accessed 7 Aug 2018].

Bughin, J., Hazan, E., Ramaswamy, S., Chui, M., Allas, T., Dahlström, P., Henke, N., and Trench, M., 2017. Artificial Intelligence The Next Digital Frontier? [online]. Available from: https://www.mckinsey.com/~/media/mckinsey/industries/advanced%20electronics/our%20insights/how%20artificial%20intelligence%20can%20deliver%20real%20value%20to%20companies/mgi-artificial-intelligence-discussion-paper.ashx [Accessed 7 Aug 2018].

Butner, K., Chawla, M., Crowther, M., Favilla, J. R., and Marshall, A., 2017. Sharpening Your Digital Edge [online]. Available from: https://public.dhe.ibm.com/common/ssi/ecm/gb/en/gbe03820usen/gbe03820usen-00_GBE03820USEN.pdf [Accessed 27 Sep 2018].

C3, 2018a. C3 [online]. Available from: https://c3iot.ai/wp-content/uploads/C3-Products-Services-Overview.pdf [Accessed 31 Oct 2018].

C3, 2018b. C3 Platform [online]. Available from: https://c3.ai/wp-content/uploads/18_1025_C3_Platform_DataSheet.pdf [Accessed 31 Oct 2018].

Carson, B., Romanelli, G., Walsh, P., and Zhumaev, A., 2018. Blockchain beyond the Hype: What is the strategic business value? [online]. Available from: https://www.mckinsey.com/~/media/McKinsey/Business%20Functions/McKinsey%20Digital/Our%20Insights/Blockchain%20beyond%20the%20hype%20What%20is%20the%20strategic%20business%20value/Blockchain-beyond-the-hype-What-is-the-strategic-business-value.ashx [Accessed 7 Aug 2018].

Chin, J. K., Hagstroem, M., Libarikian, A., and Rifai, K., 2017. Advanced Analytics [online]. Available from: https://www.mckinsey.com/~/media/McKinsey/Business%20Functions/McKinsey%20Analytics/Our%20Insights/Advanced%20analytics%20Nine%20insights%20from%20the%20C-suite/Advanced-analytics-Nine-insights-from-the-C-suite.ashx [Accessed 13 Dec 2018].

Chistty, P., 2017. Prepare for the Impact of Digital Twins [online]. Available from: https://www.gartner.com/smarterwithgartner/prepare-for-the-impact-of-digital-twins/ [Accessed 7 Aug 2018].

Chui, M., Manyika, J., and Miremadi, M., 2018. What AI Can and Can't Do (Yet) for Your Business [online]. Available from: https://www.mckinsey.com/business-functions/mckinsey-analytics/our-insights/what-ai-can-and-cant-do-yet-for-your-business [Accessed 7 Aug 2018].

Chui, M., Manyika, J., Miremadi, M., Henke, N., Chung, R., Nel, P., and Malhotra, S., 2018a. Notes from the AI Frontier: Insights from Hundreds of Use Cases [online]. Available from: https://www.mckinsey.com/~/media/McKinsey/Global%20Themes/Artificial%20I ntelligence/Notes%20from%20the%20AI%20frontier%20Applications%20and%2 0value%20of%20deep%20learning/MGI_Notes-from-AI-Frontier_Discussion-paper.ashx [Accessed 7 Oct 2018].

Chui, M., Manyika, J., Miremadi, M., Henke, N., Chung, R., Nel, P., and Malhotra, S., 2018b. Notes from the AI Frontier: Applications and Value of Deep Learning [online]. Available from: https://www.mckinsey.com/featured-insights/artificial-intelligence/notes-from-the-ai-frontier-applications-and-value-of-deep-learning#0 [Accessed 7 Oct 2018].

CIMdata, 2017a. Product Innovation Platform Assessment [online]. Available from: https://www.aras.com/papers/EBOOK-CIMdata-Aras-PLM-Platform-Evaluation.pdf [Accessed 7 Aug 2018].

CIMdata, 2017b. Product Innovation Platforms: Definition, Their Role in the Enterprise, and Their Long-Term Viability [online]. Available from: https://www.aras.com/papers/WHITE-PAPER-cimdata-product-innovation-platforms-definition.pdf [Accessed 7 Aug 2018].

Cisco, 2017. Understanding the IoT Security Ecosystem [online]. Available from: https://www.jasper.com/sites/default/files/cisco-jasper_understanding-the-iot-security-ecosystem-en.pdf [Accessed 15 Nov 2018].

Cline, G., 2017. Product Development and the Centrality of Digital Twin [online]. Available from: https://www-01.ibm.com/common/ssi/cgi-bin/ssialias?htmlfid=WWL12391USEN&) [Accessed 7 Aug 2018].

Cotteleer, M. J. and Sniderman, B., 2017. Forces of Change: Industry 4.0 [online]. Available from: https://www2.deloitte.com/content/dam/insights/us/articles/4323_Forces-of-change/4323_Forces-of-change_Ind4-0.pdf [Accessed 4 Oct 2018].

Dassault Systèmes, 2014. Apriso Smart-Pull Manufacturing Solution [online]. Available from: http://www.apriso.com/library/white_papers/Smart-Pull-Manufacturing-Solution-Brochure.pdf [Accessed 7 Aug 2018].

Dassault Systèmes, 2017a. Global Industrial Operations [online]. Available from: https://www.3ds.com/fileadmin/PRODUCTS-SERVICES/DELMIA/PDF/Brochure-DELMIA-2017.pdf [Accessed 7 Aug 2018].

Dassault Systèmes, 2017b. A Practical Guide to Transform Manufacturing Operations with Smart Pull [online]. Available from: http://www.apriso.com/library/white_papers/Apriso_WhitePaper_Beyond_Lean-Unleashing_Power_of_Pull.pdf [Accessed 7 Aug 2018].

Dassault Systèmes, 2017c. The Digital Manufacturing Enterprise: Leveraging ISA-95 as a Foundation [online]. Available from: http://www.apriso.com/library/Whitepaper_Digital_Manufacturing_Enterprise.php [Accessed 7 Aug 2018].

Dassault Systèmes, 2018. 3D Experience for Software Lifecycle Management (SWLM): A Federated Platform for Software Driven Innovation [online]. Available from: https://ifwe.3ds.com/sites/default/files/HT_3DEXPforSLM_WhitePaper.pdf [Accessed 7 Aug 2018].

Dawson, A., Hirt, M., and Scanlan, J., 2016. The Economic Essentials of Digital Strategy [online]. Available from: https://www.mckinsey.com/business-functions/strategy-and-corporate-finance/our-insights/the-economic-essentials-of-digital-strategy [Accessed 7 Oct 2018].

De Smet, A., Lackey, G., and Weiss, L. M., 2018. Untangling Your Organization's Decision Making [online]. Available from: https://www.mckinsey.com/business-functions/organization/our-insights/untangling-your-organizations-decision-making?cid=other-eml-cls-mip-mck&hlkid=b0e228c49976469a889b462900f97f2f&hctky=10322662&hdpid=0e9eb964-06e8-4caa-821f-4c0adfc79635 [Accessed 26 Nov 2018].

De Smet, A., Lurie, M., and St. George, A., 2018. Leading Agile Transformation [online]. Available from: https://www.mckinsey.com/~/media/mckinsey/business%20functions/organization/our%20insights/leading%20agile%20transformation%20the%20new%20capabilities%20leaders%20need%20to%20build/leading-agile-transformation-the-new-capabilities-leaders-need-to-build-21st-century-organizations.ashx [Accessed 8 Oct 2018].

Deloitte, 2017. From Mystery to Mastery: Unlocking the Business Value of Artificial Intelligence in the Insurance Industry [online]. Available from: https://www2.deloitte.com/content/dam/Deloitte/de/Documents/Innovation/Artificial-Intelligence-in-Insurance-Whitepaper-deloitte-digital.pdf [Accessed 7 Aug 2018].

Deloitte, 2018a. Industry 4.0: 2017 Global Impact Report [online]. Available from: https://www2.deloitte.com/content/campaigns/global/global-report/global-report.html [Accessed 7 Aug 2018].

Deloitte, 2018b. The Fourth Industrial Revolution Is Here - Are You Ready? [online]. Available from: https://www.forbes.com/forbes-insights/wp-content/uploads/2018/01/Deloitte-FourthIndustrialRev_REPORT_FINAL-WEB.pdf [Accessed 4 Oct 2018].

Device Inside, 2018. Artificial Intelligence in IoT Practice [online]. Available from: https://www.device-insight.com/en/confirmation-and-download-ai-whitepaper-2018.html?key=1b28b7c7b3b1bfb33b11600ceb458bd938ac91a6 [Accessed 2 Nov 2018].

Dhawan, R., Heid, B., Küderli, P., and Laczkowski, K., 2018. How industrial companies can respond to disruptive forces.

Dijkstra, E. and Smith, J., 2018. Being Human in a Digital World – Part 1 [online]. Available from: https://atos.net/en/blog/human-digital-world-part-1 [Accessed 24 Nov 2018].

Edlich, A., Ip, F., Panikkar, R., and Whiteman, R., 2018. The Automation Imperative [online]. Available from: https://www.mckinsey.com/business-functions/operations/our-insights/the-automation-imperative?cid=other-eml-alt-mip-mck-1810&hlkid=4ae72c6ab07f49948efcf49190e52e70&hctky=10322662&hdpid=afb9 3578-b3df-4a79-81af-bec6055a23b1 [Accessed 28 Oct 2018].

Favilla, J. R., Lin, S., Chawla, M., Dickson, D., and Kalagnanam, J., 2018. The Artificial Intelligence Effect on Industrial Products [online]. Available from: https://public.dhe.ibm.com/common/ssi/ecm/17/en/17013217usen/industrial-products-ai_17013217USEN.pdf [Accessed 31 Oct 2018].

Fleming, N., 2017. The Forrester WaveTM: Product Lifecycle Management for Discrete Manufacturers, Q4 2017: The Seven Providers That Matter Most and How They Stack Up [online]. Available from: https://www.ptc.com/-/media/Files/PDFs/PLM/Forrester-Report.pdf?la=en&hash=48DFA0884027E5AD35D7C41D405F416FE417323D [Accessed 7 Aug 2018].

Floyd, S., 2014. Product Development and Manufacturing Technology Trends [online]. Available from: https://www.aras.com/papers/SLIDES-Microsoft-PLM-Product-Development-Manufacturing-Trends.pdf [Accessed 3 Dec 2018].

Gartner, 2018. Magic Quadrant for Industrial IoT Platforms [online]. Available from: https://www.gartner.com/doc/reprints?id=1-50EOIFM&ct=180518&st=sb [Accessed 10 Nov 2018].

Gates, B., 1995. Bill Gates Quotes About Internet [online]. Available from: https://www.azquotes.com/author/5382-Bill_Gates/tag/internet [Accessed 1 Dec 2018].

General Electric, 2016. The Digital Twin: Compressing Time-to-Value for Digital Industrial Companies [online]. Available from: https://www.ge.com/digital/sites/default/files/The-Digital-Twin_Compressing-Time-to-Value-for-Digital-Industrial-Companies.pdf [Accessed 7 Aug 2018].

General Electric, 2018a. Edge Computing: Driving New Outcomes from Intelligent Industrial Machines [online]. Available from: https://www.ge.com/digital/sites/default/files/download_assets/Edge-Computing-Driving-New-Outcomes.pdf [Accessed 31 Oct 2018].

General Electric, 2018b. Consumer vs. Industrial Internet [online]. Available from: https://www.ge.com/digital/sites/default/files/download_assets/Consumer_vs_Indu strial_Internet_Infographic.pdf [Accessed 31 Oct 2018].

General Electric, 2018c. Predix [online]. Available from: https://www.ge.com/digital/sites/default/files/download_assets/Predix-The-Industrial-Internet-Platform-Brief.pdf [Accessed 31 Oct 2018].

General Electric, 2018d. Predix Manufacturing Execution Systems [online]. Available from: https://www.ge.com/digital/sites/default/files/download_assets/Predix-Manufacturing-Execution-Systems-from-GE-Digital.pdf [Accessed 31 Oct 2018].

General Electric Company, 2016. GE Digital Twin [online]. Available from: https://www.ge.com/digital/sites/default/files/Digital-Twin-for-the-digital-power-plant-.pdf [Accessed 7 Aug 2018].

Gerber, A., 2017. Connecting the Internet of Things [online]. Available from: https://www.ibm.com/developerworks/library/iot-lp101-connectivity-network-protocols/index.html [Accessed 7 Aug 2018].

Gramatke, M., Gegner, J., Bauer, S., Boenisch, M., and Le, V. D. B., 2017. Cognitive Artificial Intelligence: The Invisible Invasion of the Media Business [online]. Available from: https://www2.deloitte.com/de/de/pages/technology-media-and-telecommunications/articles/cognitive-artificial-intelligence-in-media.html [Accessed 7 Aug 2018].

Grieves, M., 2014. Digital Twin: Manufacturing Excellence through Virtual Factory Replication [online]. Available from: http://innovate.fit.edu/plm/documents/doc_mgr/912/1411.0_Digital_Twin_White_Paper_Dr_Grieves.pdf [Accessed 7 Aug 2018].

Grieves, M. and Vickers, J., 2001. Digital Twin: Mitigating Unpredictable, Undesirable Emergent Behavior in Complex Systems.

Gupta, V. and Ulrich, R., 2017. How the Internet of Things Will Reshape Future Production Systems [online]. Modern Vision. Available from: https://www.mckinsey.com/business-functions/operations/our-insights/how-the-internet-of-things-will-reshape-future-production-systems [Accessed 7 Aug 2018].

Henke, N., Bughin, J., Chui, M., Manyika, J., Saleh, T., Wiseman, B., and Sethupathy, G., 2016. The Age of Analytics [online]. Available from: https://www.mckinsey.com/~/media/McKinsey/Business%20Functions/McKinsey%20Analytics/Our%20Insights/The%20age%20of%20analytics%20Competing%20in%20a%20data%20driven%20world/MGI-The-Age-of-Analytics-Full-report.ashx [Accessed 7 Aug 2018].

Hitachi, 2018. Accelerate Your IoT Journey With Hitach is Edge-to-Outcome IoT Platform: Lumada [online]. Available from: https://www.hitachivantara.com/en-us/pdfd/solution-profile/accelerate-iot-journey-with-lumada-solution-profile.pdf [Accessed 12 Dec 2018].

Hughes, A., 2017. Jumpstart Digital Transformation with MES [online]. Available from: http://www.apriso.com/library/white_papers/JumpstartDigitalTransformationwith MES_Dassault.pdf [Accessed 7 Aug 2018].

IBM, 2017a. Watson IoT [online]. Available from: https://www.ibm.com/blogs/internet-of-things/cloud-afm-saas/ [Accessed 31 Oct 2018].

IBM, 2017b. Cognitive Catalysts [online]. Available from: https://public.dhe.ibm.com/common/ssi/ecm/gb/en/gbe03877usen/gbe03877usen-03_GBE03877USEN.pdf [Accessed 27 Sep 2018].

IBM, 2017c. Be Ready for Industry 4.0 with Cognitive Manufacturing [online]. Available from: https://public.dhe.ibm.com/common/ssi/ecm/id/en/idm12345usen/watson-iot-cognitive-solutions-ww-e-book-idm12345usen-20180502.pdf [Accessed 27 Sep 2018].

IBM, 2018a. IBM IoT Continuous Engineering [online]. Available from: https://www.ibm.com/de-en/marketplace/engineering-solutions-on-cloud/details [Accessed 12 Dec 2018].

IBM, 2018b. Enterprise Ready AI [online]. Available from: https://www.ibm.com/watson/about/ [Accessed 12 Dec 2018].

IBM, 2018c. IBM Collaborative Lifecycle Management [online]. Available from: https://jazz.net/products/clm [Accessed 15 Dec 2018].

IDC, 2017. The Next Steps in Digital Transformation [online]. Available from: https://news.sap.com/wp-content/blogs.dir/1/files/SAP_IDC_infobrief_SMB_DX_102016.pdf [Accessed 4 Oct 2018].

Industrie 4.0 Working Group, 2013. Recommendations for Implementing the Strategic Initiative INDUSTRIE 4.0 [online]. Available from: https://www.acatech.de/wp-content/uploads/2018/03/Final_report__Industrie_4.0_accessible.pdf [Accessed 7 Aug 2018].

Kaiser, T., 2016. Leveraging Digital Twins to Breathe New Life into Your Products and Services [online]. Available from: https://www.digitalistmag.com/iot/2016/10/12/digital-twins-breathe-new-life-into-products-and-services-04572599 [Accessed 7 Aug 2018].

Kuehn, W., 1994. Object Oriented Approach for the Integrated Modeling of Manufacturing Systems. Presented at the New Directions in Simulation for Manufacturing and Communications, Tokyo, Japan, 428–433.

Levene, J., Litman, S., Schillinger, I., and Toomey, C., 2018. How Advanced Analytics Can Benefit Infrastructure Capital Planning [online]. Available from: https://www.mckinsey.com/~/media/McKinsey/Industries/Capital%20Projects%20and%20Infrastructure/Our%20Insights/How%20advanced%20analytics%20can%20benefit%20infrastructure%20capital%20planning/How-advanced-analytics-can-benefit-infrastructure-capital-planning.ashx [Accessed 7 Aug 2018].

LNS Research, 2018. MOM and PLM in the IIoT Age [online]. Available from: http://www.apriso.com/library/white_papers/MOMandPLMintheIIOTAge.pdf [Accessed 7 Aug 2018].

LoRa Alliance, 2015. LoRaWAN [online]. Available from: https://lora-alliance.org/sites/default/files/2018-04/what-is-lorawan.pdf [Accessed 9 Aug 2018].

Lowes, P., Cannata, F. R. S., Chitre, S., and Barkham, J., 2017. Service Delivery Transformation: Automate This [online]. Available from: https://www2.deloitte.com/content/dam/Deloitte/us/Documents/process-and-operations/us-sdt-process-automation.pdf [Accessed 7 Aug 2018].

Lucas, S., 2016a. Introducing the SAP Digital Enterprise Platform [online]. Available from: https://blogs.saphana.com/2016/01/11/the-sap-digital-enterprise-platform-part-1-delivering-connected-infrastructure-insight-to-drive-the-digital-enterprise/ [Accessed 4 Oct 2018].

Lucas, S., 2016b. The Benefits of the SAP Digital Enterprise Platform - SAP HANA [online]. Available from: https://blogs.saphana.com/2016/02/03/the-benefits-of-the-sap-digital-enterprise-platform/.

MacGillivray, C., 2018. How Data Is Fueling Digital Transformation and Changing the Role of IoT [online]. Available from: https://www.iot-data-drives-dx.com/thank-you.

machineQ, 2018. Enabling Wide Area IoT Solutions with machineQ, a Comcast Service [online]. Available from: https://info.semtech.com/hubfs/WHITE-PAPER_Enabling-Wide-Area-IoT-Solutions-with-machineQ-1-1.pdf [Accessed 9 Aug 2018].

Manyika, J., 2017. What's Now and Next in Analytics, AI, and Automation [online]. Available from: https://www.mckinsey.com/~/media/mckinsey/global%20themes/digital%20disruption/whats%20now%20and%20next%20in%20analytics%20automation/final%20pdf/mgi-briefing-note-automation-final.ashx [Accessed 7 Aug 2018].

Manyika, J., Chui, M., Miremadi, M., Bughin, J., George, K., Willmott, P., and Dewhurst, M., 2017. A Future that Works: Automation, Employment, and Productivity [online]. Available from: https://www.mckinsey.com/mgi/overview/2017-in-review/automation-and-the-future-of-work/a-future-that-works-automation-employment-and-productivity [Accessed 7 Aug 2018].

Mayer, E., 2017. IBM Continuous Engineering [online]. Available from: https://www.aras.com/papers/SLIDES-ibm-augmenting-plm-alm-systems-engineering.pdf [Accessed 7 Aug 2018].

McDermott, B., 2018. Machines Can't Dream [online]. Available from: https://news.sap.com/impact-of-artificial-intelligence-machines-cant-dream/ [Accessed 7 Aug 2018].

McKinsey, 2017a. Smartening Up with Artificial Intelligence (AI) [online]. Available from: https://www.mckinsey.com/~/media/McKinsey/Industries/Semiconductors/Our%2 0Insights/Smartening%20up%20with%20artificial%20intelligence/Smartening-up-with-artificial-intelligence.ashx [Accessed 7 Aug 2018].

McKinsey, 2017b. An Executive's Guide to AI [online]. Available from: https://www.mckinsey.com/business-functions/mckinsey-analytics/our-insights/an-executives-guide-to-ai [Accessed 7 Aug 2018].

McKinsey, 2018. Disruptive Forces in the Industrial Sectors [online]. Available from: https://www.mckinsey.com/~/media/McKinsey/Industries/Automotive%20and%20 Assembly/Our%20Insights/How%20industrial%20companies%20can%20respond %20to%20disruptive%20forces/Disruptive-forces-in-the-industrial-sectors.ashx [Accessed 7 Aug 2018].

Menard, A., 2018. How Can We Recognize the Real Power of the Internet of Things? [online]. Available from: https://www.mckinsey.com/business-functions/digital-mckinsey/our-insights/how-can-we-recognize-the-real-power-of-the-internet-of-things [Accessed 7 Aug 2018].

Microsoft, 2018. Adopting the Microsoft Cloud Operating Model [online]. Available from: https://azure.microsoft.com/mediahandler/files/resourcefiles/cloud-operating-model---full-document/FINAL-Cloud%20Operating%20Model.pdf [Accessed 9 Nov 2018].

Mikell, M. and Clark, J., 2018. Digital Twin: Cheat Sheet: What is Digital Twin? [online]. Available from: https://www.ibm.com/blogs/internet-of-things/iot-cheat-sheet-digital-twin/ [Accessed 7 Aug 2018].

Miller, P. and Pelino, M., 2018. The Forrester WaveTM: Industrial IoT Software Platforms, Q3 2018 [online]. Available from: https://public.dhe.ibm.com/common/ssi/ecm/04/en/04018604usen/forrester-wave-for-iiot-platforms-report-for-website_04018604USEN.pdf [Accessed 31 Oct 2018].

Mussomeli, A., Gish, D., and Laaper, S., 2016. The Rise of the Digital Supply Network [online]. Available from: https://www2.deloitte.com/content/dam/insights/us/articles/3465_Digital-supply-network/DUP_Digital-supply-network.pdf [Accessed 4 Oct 2018].

Oracle, 2012. Oracle Enterprise Product Lifecycle Management [online]. Available from: https://www.oracle.com/us/assets/enterp-prod-lifecycle-manag-rept-1621419.pdf [Accessed 7 Aug 2018].

Oracle, 2016a. Driving Real-Time Insight [online]. Available from: http://www.oracle.com/us/solutions/internetofthings/big-data-and-iot-wp-3098381.pdf [Accessed 7 Aug 2018].

Oracle, 2016b. Oracle Internet of Things Cloud Service [online]. Available from: http://www.oracle.com/us/solutions/internetofthings/iot-cloud-service-ds-3209769.pdf [Accessed 7 Aug 2018].

Oracle, 2017. Digital Twins for IoT Applications [online]. Available from: http://www.oracle.com/us/solutions/internetofthings/digital-twins-for-iot-apps-wp-3491953.pdf [Accessed 7 Aug 2018].

Osan, A. and Somers, K., 2017. Optimizing Production in the Age of the Machine [online]. Available from: https://www.mckinsey.com/business-functions/operations/our-insights/optimizing-production-in-the-age-of-the-machine [Accessed 7 Aug 2018].

Panetta, K., 2016. Gartner's Top 10 Strategic Technology Trends for 2017 [online]. Available from: https://www.gartner.com/smarterwithgartner/gartners-top-10-technology-trends-2017/ [Accessed 7 Aug 2018].

Panetta, K., 2017. Gartner Top 10 Strategic Technology Trends for 2018 [online]. Available from: https://www.gartner.com/smarterwithgartner/gartner-top-10-strategic-technology-trends-for-2018/ [Accessed 7 Aug 2018].

Panetta, K., 2018. Gartner Top 10 Strategic Technology Trends for 2019 [online]. Available from: https://www.gartner.com/smarterwithgartner/gartner-top-10-strategic-technology-trends-for-2019/.

Parris, C. J., Laflen, B., Grabb, M. L., and Kalitan, D. M., 2016. The Future of Industrial Services: The Digital Twin [online]. Available from: https://www.infosys.com/insights/services-being-digital/Documents/future-industrial-digital.pdf [Accessed 7 Aug 2018].

Parrott, A. and Warshaw, L., 2017. Industry 4.0 and the Digital Twin [online]. Available from: https://www2.deloitte.com/insights/us/en/focus/industry-4-0/digital-twin-technology-smart-factory.html [Accessed 7 Aug 2018].

Porter, M. E. and Heppelmann, J. E., 2015. How Smart, Connected Products Are Transforming Companies [online]. Harvard Business Review. Available from: https://www.ptc.com/-/media/Files/PDFs/IoT/HBR-How-Smart-Connected-Products-Are-Transforming-Companies.pdf [Accessed 7 Aug 2018].

Porter, M. E. and Heppelmann, J. E., 2017. A Manager's Guide to Augmented Reality [online]. Harvard Business Review. Available from: https://www.ptc.com/-/media/Files/PDFs/Augmented-Reality/HBR-Managers-Guide-to-AR.pdf [Accessed 7 Aug 2018].

Pronier, J.-Y., 2018. Unlocking Business Advantage with Digital Twins [online]. Available from: https://blog.vantiq.com/real-time-enterprise/unlocking-business-advantage-with-digital-twins [Accessed 20 Dec 2018].

ProSTEP iViP, 2015. Code of PLM Openness (CPO) [online]. Available from: https://www.prostep.org/fileadmin/CPO/ProSTEP-iViP_CPO_V14_151019.pdf [Accessed 6 Nov 2018].

PTC, 2017. Thingworx Navigate: Transform Product Development with Easy Access to PLM [online]. Available from: https://www.ptc.com/-/media/Files/PDFs/Navigate/ThingWorx_Navigate_ebk.pdf?la=en&hash=5F52EF5155D0BFD18A4244C462B7216747AE171E [Accessed 7 Aug 2018].

Rahi, R., 2017. Oracle Cloud Infrastructure [online]. Available from: http://www.oracle.com/technetwork/architect/cloud-infra-arch-wp.pdf [Accessed 7 Aug 2018].

SAP, 2017. SAP Digital Transformation Executive Study.

SAP, 2018a. What is Machine Learning? [online]. Available from: https://www.sap.com/products/leonardo/machine-learning/what-is-machine-learning.html [Accessed 7 Aug 2018].

SAP, 2018b. SAP Leonardo [online]. Available from: https://www.sap.com/products/leonardo.html#pdf-asset=e033a960-057d-0010-87a3-c30de2ffd8ff&page=1 [Accessed 26 Nov 2018].

SAP, 2018c. SAP S/4HANA Cloud [online]. Available from: https://www.sap.com/products/s4hana-erp-cloud.html [Accessed 26 Nov 2018].

Schofield, J., 2011. Ken Olsen Obituary [online]. Available from: https://www.theguardian.com/technology/2011/feb/09/ken-olsen-obituary [Accessed 1 Dec 2018].

Schuh, G., Anderl, R., Gausemeier, J., Hompel, M. T., and Wahlster, W., 2017. Industrie 4.0 Maturity Index: Managing the Digital Transformation of Companies [online]. Available from: https://www.ptc.com/-/media/Files/PDFs/IoT/acatech_STUDIE_Maturity_Index_eng_WEB.PDF [Accessed 7 Aug 2018].

Schwartz, J., Stockton, H., and Monahan, K., 2017. Forces of Change [online]. Available from: https://www2.deloitte.com/insights/us/en/focus/technology-and-the-future-of-work/overview.html [Accessed 4 Oct 2018].

Sharma, A.-M., 2018. Industrie 4.0 [online]. Available from: https://www.gtai.de/GTAI/Navigation/EN/Invest/Industries/Industrie-4-0/Industrie-4-0/industrie-4-0-what-is-it.html?view=renderPdf [Accessed 4 Oct 2018].

Shetty, S., 2017. How to Use Digital Twins in Your IoT Strategy [online]. Available from: https://www.gartner.com/smarterwithgartner/how-to-use-digital-twins-in-your-iot-strategy/ [Accessed 7 Aug 2018].

Siemens, 2016. Industrial Security: Security Concept for Process and Discrete Industries [online]. Available from: https://www.siemens.com/content/dam/webassetpool/mam/tag-siemens-com/smdb/digital-factory/industrial-security/online/documents/whitepapers/en/whitepaper-security-2016-v10-en.pdf [Accessed 7 Aug 2018].

Siemens, 2017a. Manufacturing Operations Management [online]. Available from: https://w3.siemens.com/mcms/mes/en/mes_suites/Documents/Siemens-PLM-Software-solutions-for-Manufacturing-Operations-Management-brochure.pdf [Accessed 4 Oct 2018].

Siemens, 2017b. If it's high-end, it's SIMOTION [online]. Available from: https://c4b.gss.siemens.com/resources/images/articles/dffa-b10333-00-7600.pdf [Accessed 10 Sep 2018].

Siemens, 2017c. TIA Portal V15 Engineering Framework: Focus on Applications, Digitalization and Efficiency [online]. Available from: https://www.siemens.com/press/en/pressrelease/?press=/en/pressrelease/2018/corp orate/pr2018020169coen.htm&content[]=Corp&content[]=DF&content[]=PD&con tent_0=Corp&content_1=DF&content_2=PD&sheet=7 [Accessed 7 Aug 2018].

Siemens, 2017d. MindSphere [online]. Available from: http://images.siemensplmevents.com/Web/Siemens/%7Bcf7a51cf-5a8a-4249-af64-f68b2b1158a6%7D_MindSphere-Whitepaper.pdf?stc=wwiia420000 [Accessed 7 Aug 2018].

Siemens, 2017e. OPC UA [online]. Available from: https://www.siemens.com/content/dam/webassetpool/mam/tag-siemens-com/smdb/digital-factory/profinet/pdf/3-56797-dffa-b10293-01-7600-160707-opc-ua-flyer-en.pdf [Accessed 7 Aug 2018].

Siemens, 2017f. SIMATIC Energy Manager PRO [online]. Available from: https://c4b.gss.siemens.com/resources/images/articles/dffa-b10256-01-7600.pdf [Accessed 4 Oct 2018].

Siemens, 2017g. Your Gateway to Automation in the Digital Enterprise [online]. Available from: https://www.siemens.com/content/dam/webassetpool/mam/tag-siemens-com/smdb/digital-factory/totally-integrated-automation-tia/tia-portal/online/documents/tia-portal-ipdf-dffa-b10461-00-7600-en.pdf [Accessed 30 Oct 2018].

Siemens, 2018. Press Pictures [online]. Available from: https://www.siemens.com/press/en/presspicture/index.php.

Siemens, 2018a. Digital Innovation for Business Transformation [online]. Available from: https://www.plm.automation.siemens.com/global/en/our-story/vision-digital-innovation/ [Accessed 27 Sep 2018].

Siemens, 2018b. Future of Manufacturing [online]. Available from: https://www.siemens.com/global/en/home/company/innovation/pictures-of-the-future/fom.html [Accessed 7 Aug 2018].

Siemens, 2018c. Future of Manufacturing/Digital Enterprise Suite [online]. Available from: https://www.siemens.com/global/en/home/company/topic-areas/future-of-manufacturing/digital-enterprise.html [Accessed 7 Aug 2018].

Siemens, 2018d. Digital Innovation: Business Transformation to Realize Innovation [online]. Available from: https://www.plm.automation.siemens.com/global/de/our-story/vision-digital-innovation/ [Accessed 7 Aug 2018].

Siemens, 2018e. Unlock the Potential with Digitalization: Innovations at Siemens [online]. Available from: https://www.siemens.com/global/en/home/company/innovation/pictures-of-the-future/innovations.html [Accessed 7 Aug 2018].

Siemens, 2018f. Digital Innovation Platform [online]. Available from: https://www.plm.automation.siemens.com/global/en/our-story/vision-digital-innovation/digital-innovation-platform.html [Accessed 30 Oct 2018].

Siemens, 2018g. Press Pictures [online]. Available from: https://www.siemens.com/press/en/presspicture/index.php.

Siemens, 2018h. Additive Manufacturing: The Future is 3D [online]. Available from: https://new.siemens.com/global/en/company/innovation/pictures-of-the-future/additive-manufacturing.html.

Siemens, 2018i. Siemens Launches Additive Manufacturing Network to Transform Global Manufacturing [online]. Available from: https://www.siemens.com/press/en/pressrelease/?press=/en/pressrelease/2018/corporate/pr2018020169coen.htm&content[]=Corp&content[]=DF&content[]=PD [Accessed 7 Aug 2018].

Siemens, 2018j. Protecting Productivity: Industrial Security [online]. Available from: https://www.siemens.com/content/dam/webassetpool/mam/tag-siemens-com/smdb/digital-factory/industrial-security/online/documents/broschueren/en/tuev-flyer-en-dffa-b10334-00-7600.pdf [Accessed 7 Aug 2018].

Siemens, 2018k. Increased Productivity for Machine Tools and Motion Control Drive Systems with MindApps [online]. Available from: https://www.siemens.com/press/en/pressrelease/?press=/en/pressrelease/2018/corporate/pr2018020169coen.htm&content[]=Corp&content[]=DF&content[]=PD&content_0=Corp&content_1=DF&content_2=PD&sheet=1 [Accessed 7 Aug 2018].

Siemens, 2018l. MindSphere [online]. Available from: https://www.siemens.com/content/dam/webassetpool/mam/tag-siemens-com/smdb/corporate-core/software/mindsphere/mindsphere-brochure.pdf [Accessed 30 Oct 2018].

Siemens PLM Software, 2018. Defining Closed-Loop Manufacturing [online]. Available from: http://www.mesa.org/en/resourcelibrary/resources/Smart-Story/Siemens-PLM-Defining-Closed-loop-manufacturing-wp-71314-A4.pdf [Accessed 30 Oct 2018].

Sniderman, B., Mahto, M., and Cotteleer, M. J., 2016. Industry 4.0 and Manufacturing Ecosystems [online]. Available from: https://www2.deloitte.com/content/dam/insights/us/articles/manufacturing-ecosystems-exploring-world-connected-enterprises/DUP_2898_Industry4.0ManufacturingEcosystems.pdf [Accessed 7 Aug 2018].

SoftwareAG, 2018a. How to Create the Right Hybrid Integration Strategy [online]. Available from: https://resources.softwareag.com/integration/hybrid-integration-in-era-of-digital-disruption-white-paper.

SoftwareAG, 2018b. Predictive Maintenance for Manufacturing [online]. Available from: https://resources.softwareag.com/industry-ebooks/predictive-maintenance-services-smart-manufacturing-iot-fact-sheet.

Systems, W. R. Oracle, 2016. Extending Enterprise to the Edge [online]. Available from: http://www.oracle.com/us/solutions/internetofthings/driving-digital-transformation-3221500.pdf [Accessed 7 Aug 2018].

The Open Group, 2018. Service-Oriented Architecture – What Is SOA? [online]. Available from: http://www.opengroup.org/soa/source-book/soa/p1.htm [Accessed 12 Dec 2018].

Tierney, B., 2017. Building an Adaptive Intelligence Process in Oracle Cloud [online]. Available from: http://www.oracle.com/technetwork/articles/cloudcomp/building-adaptive-intel-process-3843180.html [Accessed 7 Aug 2018].

Tilley, J., 2017. Automation, Robotics, and the Factory of the Future [online]. Available from: https://www.mckinsey.com/business-functions/operations/our-insights/automation-robotics-and-the-factory-of-the-future [Accessed 7 Aug 2018].

Tressel, J., van der Veen, J., and Heeneman, T., 2017. Perspektiv Part 4: Five Technologies Trends that Leap-frog Artificial Intelligence [online]. Available from: https://www2.deloitte.com/se/sv/pages/technology/articles/part4-five-technologies-trends-that-leap-frog-artificial-intelligence.html [Accessed 8 Dec 2018].

Turner, V., 2016. Reducing the Time to Value for Internet of Things Deployments [online]. Available from: https://www.oracle.com/webfolder/s/delivery_production/docs/FY16h1/doc25/IDC WhitePaperFinal.pdf [Accessed 7 Aug 2018].

Turner, V. and MacGillivray, C., 2017. IDC FutureScape: Worldwide IoT 2018 Predictions [online]. Available from: https://www.idc.com/getdoc.jsp?containerId=US43193617 [Accessed 7 Aug 2018].

Vermeulen, B. and Pyka, A., 2016. Agent-based Modeling for Decision Making in Economics under Uncertainty. Economics: The Open-Access, Open-Assessment E-Journal [online], (2). Available from: http://www.economics-ejournal.org/economics/journalarticles/2016-6.

Wasserman, S., 2017. What Is the Digital Twin and Why Should Simulation and IoT Experts Care? [online]. Available from: https://www.engineering.com/DesignSoftware/DesignSoftwareArticles/ArticleID/16070/What-is-the-Digital-Twin-and-Why-Should-Simulation-and-IoT-Experts-Care.aspx [Accessed 7 Aug 2018].

Wellers, D., Woods, J., Jendroska, D., and Koch, C., 2017. Why Machine Learning and Why Now? [online]. Available from: https://www.sap.com/documents/2017/05/de7cfb6d-b97c-0010-82c7-eda71af511fa.html [Accessed 7 Aug 2018].

White, G. R. T., 2017. Future Applications of Blockchain in Business and Management. Strategic Change, 26 (5), 439–451.

Williams, D. D. and Allen, I. L., 2017. Using Artificial Intelligence to Optimize the
    Value of Robotic Process Automation [online]. Available from:
    https://public.dhe.ibm.com/common/ssi/ecm/gb/en/gbw03394usen/gbw03394usen-
    03_GBW03394USEN.pdf [Accessed 31 Oct 2018].
Willmott, P., 2013. The Digital Enterprise [online]. Available from:
    https://www.mckinsey.com/business-functions/digital-mckinsey/our-insights/the-
    digital-enterprise [Accessed 9 Oct 2018].

Index

Printed in the United States
By Bookmasters